DESIGNING AND USING DATABASES FOR SCHOOL IMPROVEMENT

VICTORIA L. BERNHARDT, Ph.D.

Executive Director

Education for the Future Initiative

Professor

Department of Professional Studies in Education

College of Communication and Education

California State University, Chico, CA

EYE ON EDUCATION

EYE ON EDUCATION
6 DEPOT WAY WEST
LARCHMONT, NY 10538
(914) 833-0551
(914) 833-0761 Fax

For information about permission to reproduce selections from this book, write:
Eye On Education
Permission Dept.
6 Depot Way West
Larchmont, NY 10538

Library of Congress Cataloging—in—Publication Data

Bernhardt, Victoria L., 1952-
    Designing and using databases / by Victoria L. Bernhardt.
        p. cm.
    Includes bibliographical references.
    ISBN 1-883001-95-1
    1. Computer managed instruction--United States. 2. Database design--United States.
    3. Education--United States--Data processing. 4. School improvement programs--United
States. I. Title.

    LB1028.46.B48 2000
    370'.285--dc21   00-023823

10 9 8 7 6 5 4 3 2

Staff Development: Practices that Promote Leadership in Learning Communities
By Sally J. Zepeda

Implementation: Making Things Happen
By Anita M. Pankake

Self Efficacy: Raising the Bar for Students with Learning Needs
By Eisenberger, Conti-D'Antonio, and Bertrando

The Directory of Programs for Students at Risk
by Thomas L. Williams

Banishing Anonymity: Middle and High School Advisement Programs
By John M. Jenkins and Bonnie S. Daniel

Personalized Instruction: Changing Classroom Practice
By James Keefe and John Jenkins

The Paideia Classroom: Teaching for Understanding
By Terry Roberts with Laura Billings

The Interdisciplinary Curriculum
By Arthur K. Ellis and Carol J. Stuen

Collaborative Learning in Middle and Secondary Schools
by Dawn M. Snodgrass and Mary M. Bevevino

Transforming Schools into Community Learning Centers
By Steve R. Parson

Best Practices from America's Middle Schools
By Charles R. Watson

Research on Educational Innovations 2/e
By Arthur K. Ellis and Jeffrey T. Fouts

Action Research on Block Scheduling
By David Marshak

The Educator's Brief Guide to the Internet and the World Wide Web
By Eugene F. Provenzo, Jr.

Instruction and the Learning Environment
By James Keefe and John Jenkins

Foreign Language Teacher's Guide to Active Learning
By Deborah Blaz

ACKNOWLEDGEMENTS

I wish to acknowledge the people who have helped to make this book factual and useful. A special thanks to my "super" reviewers: Peter Waldschmidt, John Greene, Mike Szymczuk, Derek Mitchell, Barry Floyd, and Andy Mark, some of whom went through this book three and four times.

Much appreciation and thanks goes to reviewers from California, Ohio, Missouri, Michigan, Iowa, South Carolina, Vermont, Texas, New York, and Arizona who helped me to improve this product: Bob Birdsell, George Bonilla, Dave Buell, Jo Campbell, Sue Clayton, Barbara Conklin, Laura Dearden, Carol Duley, Judy English, Sam Ewing, Doug Gillum, Pat Gopperton, Irma Hernandez, Pete Higgins, Dan Hunsberger, James Jones, Kurt Larsen, Marcy Lauck, Mary Leslie, Chris Lester, Mark Maynard, Jeanne Miyasaka, Harley North, Paul Preuss, Judi Scholten, Elaine Skeete, Nancy Todd, Zana Vincent, Leni von Blanckensee, Louise Waters, Alison Watson, and Sharon Yates.

Once again, I am indebted to Lynn Varicelli for her careful and artistic work on the manuscript layout. Her dedication to her work and the work of the Education for the Future Initiative is inspiring to us all. Thank you, too, to Deborah Furgason and Marlene Trapp who assisted with early and late revisions and drafts—and to the entire staff at Education for the Future who help schools, every day, do this hard work. Bob Sickles, Publisher, Eye on Education, as usual, was wonderful to work with and especially patient with me on this book that took a little longer than the others to finish.

Without the infrastructure support of the SBC Foundation[1] we would not have the opportunity to disseminate this work across the country. I continue to marvel at the wonderful opportunities this company has given me over the years. Thank you Mary Leslie and Gloria Delgado for your continued support.

Of course, I would not be able to use those every spare minutes to write without the support of my husband, Jim Richmond.

Designing and Using Databases for School Improvement is dedicated to all hard-working educators who assist schools and school districts, daily, in using data to continuously improve education for all children.

---

[1] The SBC Foundation, along with the Southwestern Bell, Pacific Bell, Nevada Bell, SNET, and Ameritech Foundations, is the charitable foundation of SBC Communications and its family of companies, including Southwestern Bell, Pacific Bell, Nevada Bell, SNET, Ameritech, and Cellular One properties.

ABOUT THE AUTHOR

Victoria L. Bernhardt, Ph.D., is Executive Director of the Education for the Future Initiative, and Professor in the Department of Professional Studies in Education at California State University, Chico. Dr. Bernhardt received a Ph.D. in Educational Psychology Research and Measurement, with a minor in Mathematics, from the University of Oregon. Her B.S. and M.S. degrees are from Iowa State University in the fields of statistics and psychology.

Dr. Bernhardt has directed the Education for the Future Initiative since 1991. While working with schools in the Initiative, she developed the concept of the school portfolio. In 1996, this work was named one of the top three Business-Education Partnerships in the World when it received the NOVA Corporation Global Best Award for Educational Renewal and Economic Development. Dr. Bernhardt was the recipient of the 1995 McKee Foods Corporate Award for Partnership Leaders. In addition to receiving two dozen other awards, she has made numerous presentations at professional meetings and has conducted hundreds of workshops on the school portfolio and data analysis processes at local, regional, state, national, and international levels.

The author has written three companion books to this book on databases. *The School Portfolio: A Comprehensive Framework for School Improvement,* Second Edition, was written to disseminate the research behind the school portfolio. It assists schools with clarifying the purpose and vision of their learning organizations. It measures and ensures congruence of all parts of the organization to enable the attainment of their vision. *Data Analysis for Comprehensive Schoolwide Improvement*, was written to help learning organizations use data analysis to inform them of where they are, where they want to be, and how to get there—sensibly and painlessly. A third book, *The Example School Portfolio—A Companion to the School Portfolio: A Comprehensive Framework for School Improvement*, co-authored by Dr. Bernhardt and her associates, demonstrates the uses of the school portfolio as a continuous improvement tool and provides support for schools as they design and create their own school portfolio.

TABLE OF CONTENTS

FOREWORD

SBC Foundation[1], the philanthropic arm of SBC Communications, has pledged its support to education and technology issues for many years, realizing that an investment in the communities it serves is an investment in the company's own future. Our enthusiasm and support for educational initiatives and programs is fostered by a desire to connect our communities and the world with opportunities for growth and success. From our volunteer efforts to wire schools for Internet access to our financial support for scholarship programs and technology centers in low-income or rural areas, SBC has continued to look for ways to bridge the digital divide between those with access to technology and those without, through the powerful vehicle of education.

While the need for technology in education typically leads schools to search for ways of putting computers in front of students, there is another element to the use of technology that can make the difference between schools that understand and assess the needs of their students and those that do not: effective use of databases and data analysis.

Technology provides us with a helpful tool for gathering, sorting and analyzing data about our students and our educational systems. But schools must use this data to improve student learning, before technology in the classroom can provide an effective solution. Educators who create and maintain effective databases are several steps ahead in their efforts to effect change in the educational system.

The forerunner to this book, *Data Analysis for Comprehensive Schoolwide Improvement*, encouraged educators to rethink the "business" of education, analyzing data to reform and reengineer schools in a way

---

[1] The SBC Foundation, along with the Southwestern Bell, Pacific Bell, Nevada Bell, SNET, and Ameritech Foundations, is the charitable foundation of SBC Communications and its family of companies, including Southwestern Bell, Pacific Bell, Nevada Bell, SNET, Ameritech, and Cellular One properties.

---

that allows them to decide not only what to change but how to institutionalize change that will last.

Designing and Using Databases for School Improvement provides educators and school administrators with information about creating the tools they need to perform successful analysis. Author, Victoria L. Bernhardt explains the steps necessary for making data work for schools by providing, in a conversational style, guidance on the selection, design, maintenance and use of databases.

As our world becomes increasingly global, students will be required to compete for jobs and resources with increasingly sophisticated peers. Schools must provide these students with a foundation on which they can build their careers. Through the use of properly designed databases, schools can improve on the educational process and measure the effectiveness of their efforts. This book provides an invaluable start to that process. SBC is proud to support such efforts, which will benefit our communities as we prepare the next generation for the future.

Gloria Delgado
President
SBC Foundation
San Antonio, Texas

FOREWORD

TetraData Corporation, a software and services company focused on assessment and improvement in education, is very proud to be associated with Victoria L. Bernhardt, one of the finest minds and dedicated individuals that we have met in the education market space. Our firm began an independent and parallel path from Dr. Bernhardt but unknowingly shared a similar passion, i.e. that data analysis software could be made available to education executives that would facilitate the process of analyzing myriads of data relevant to the learning mission in order to make it possible for objective education-enhancement decisions to be made in a timely manner. Our paths finally crossed in 1999 and TetraData has found, in Dr. Bernhardt, a soul mate in its mission to effect education improvement.

This first edition of *Designing and Using Databases for School Improvement* identifies and explains the very fundamental issues involved with establishing and operating an education database or data warehouse. This edition aptly outlines the steps necessary to structure and build a relevant education database. It approaches the mission from both the technological perspective, i.e. the infrastructure needed, as well as, the human perspective, i.e. how to build and use the database. The entire book maintains the consistent focus of Dr. Bernhardt's primary aim, i.e. school improvement, but does so by equipping educators with the information required to build and utilize a data rich environment.

Dr. Bernhardt has delivered a principle that is pertinent to education, communities, businesses and even our personal lives. This principle is that the quality of our decisions and ensuing results will be dramatically improved if we properly utilize relevant information in the decision-making process. Very often important decision-impacting data exists but we cannot use it because we cannot access it. Dr. Bernhardt takes us beyond this inherent barrier and opens the door of opportunity for society, and especially educators, to benefit from the vast array of useful information that is available.

Armed with accurate information, Dr. Bernhardt advocates that educators will lessen the uncertainties, time and finances needed to improve educational performance and can turn education energy into results-oriented efforts. This is a message that our society has been desirous of realizing and her approach of bringing focus to education decisions and initiatives rings true and timely.

This fine work touches the needs of numerous individuals in the education network, from the teacher who needs to understand the demographics and capabilities of her individual students to school principals, district executives, regional support personnel and state and national authorities who guide the initiatives of our vast educational efforts. By virtue of her excellent skills Dr. Bernhardt has given everyone in education, including the non-technologists among us, the opportunity to benefit from this fine edition. I encourage your reading of this newest work and welcome you to embrace the passion of improving education by making objective education-enhancement decisions.

Martin S. Brutosky
Chairman and CEO
TetraData Corporation
1200 Woodruff Road, Suite A-16
Greenville, South Carolina 29607
Tel (864) 458-8243
http://www.tetradata.com

PREFACE

This book on designing and using databases for school improvement evolved from a series of data analysis workshops which were conducted around the United States for the past several years by the staff of the Education for the Future Initiative. While we have been passionate about effectively using data analysis for comprehensive school improvement and have been able to transfer that passion to other educators, we have found that school personnel are still finding it difficult to produce analyses that pinpoint what to improve and how to achieve it. Educators are "hung up" on data gathering and processing—i.e., understanding how to get the appropriate data, knowing how to get the data to "work" for them, understanding what the data suggest, and using the data to improve educational practices. Often the required data, such as individual student achievement, are not available for educators. Here we are into a new millennium, and yet very few schools have access to information (e.g., student achievement databases) that could assist them with school improvement.

I believe we are at the same point with school and district databases that we were a decade ago with the use of technology in schools. We will eventually need to gulp twice and hire appropriate personnel to support our database work, just like we had to hire technology specialists to help us set up and maintain our computers and networks.

These statements are not meant to demean the efforts of schools to use data, but rather to clarify where we are nationwide with this issue. The primary purpose of this book is to help school and district personnel understand the processes of designing and using databases for comprehensive data analyses that can be translated into classroom and school improvement, and ultimately to use these data to influence student learning in positive ways.

Designing and Using Databases for School Improvement provides a foundation for the work that helps us continuously improve everything we do for students. It explains how to:

 ◆ define the scope of the needed database
 ◆ ready the data for a database designer (official and unofficial)
 ◆ establish data analyses that will help schools improve
 ◆ and use data to continuously improve schools

Although the intent of this book is not to tell anyone what database computer software program to buy, the steps required to build a database and a tool to assist with the purchasing of database solutions are included to help "homegrown" database designers think through the steps in building a database that will lead to school improvement. While I don't purport to be a professional database designer, I find myself assisting personnel in schools and small school districts to develop their own databases so they can collect the information they need and want in order to conduct data analyses for school improvement. My personal mission is to support educational professionals in their quest for data they need and to help them use data effectively to improve their delivery of services to children. This book should help any school or district get started on designing and using databases.

Intended Audience

The intended audiences for this book are school and district administrators and teachers who want to use data to continuously improve what they do for children, colleges and university professors who teach school administrators, and support personnel who teach graduate level education courses. It is my belief that all professional educators must learn how to use data in this time of high-stakes accountability.

Designing and Using Databases for School Improvement works hand-in-glove with three previously published books—*The School Portfolio: A Comprehensive Framework for School Improvement*; *Data Analysis for Comprehensive Schoolwide Improvement*; and *The Example School Portfolio, A Companion to the School Portfolio: A Comprehensive Framework for Schoolwide Improvement*.

The School Portfolio: A Comprehensive Framework for School Improvement describes a framework for school improvement that supports the efforts of educators as they align school processes and programs with the guiding principles of the school.

Data Analysis for Comprehensive Schoolwide Improvement describes the multiple variables of data required for understanding the results the schools are getting based on the processes they are implementing.

The Example School Portfolio, A Companion to the School Portfolio: A Comprehensive Framework for Schoolwide Improvement is a prototype of a real school portfolio with three consecutive years of school data. In addition to providing insights about the way the sections work together to lead to systemic change, the authors offer practical advice about how to work with staff to get the work done efficiently and effectively.

I hope you find *Designing and Using Databases for School Improvement* to be helpful as you work through the processes of using data to improve student learning.

Victoria L. Bernhardt
Executive Director
Education for the Future
400 West First Street
Chico, CA 95929-0230
Tel (530) 898-4482
Fax (530) 898-4484
vbernhardt@csuchico.edu
http://eff.csuchico.edu

1

INTRODUCTION
The Need for a Database for Schoolwide Improvement

A superintendent I know spoke for 99 percent of the school districts in America today when he told me that his district had systems to manage money down to the dime, but no systems to manage the learning mission. This is the most critical challenge for school districts to meet.

Larry Lezotte
Learning for All

What do we want students to learn and how are we using data to measure whether learning is taking place? How do these data motivate teachers to provide appropriate instructional practices at all levels for all students? What structures are in place to support teachers and school administrators in understanding student achievement, aligning curriculum with standards, and continually using data for school improvement?

A school's effective use of data can enable the successful identification and implementation of appropriate strategies that ultimately lead to the attainment of standards and increases in student learning. However, many schools do not use data to promote increased student learning or for standards implementation. The reasons for this are varied. The data may not be easy to access, they may not be in forms that are easy to understand, no one may be available who understands and can work with data, or teachers just might not know that the data exist. For some, there may be so much data that knowing where to begin an analysis of the data is the challenge. Each of these situations (as well as many others) actively discourages schools from learning about the phenomena they are attempting to understand. By supporting the creation or access of student databases containing individual student achievement records, efforts by school leaders to create and sustain professional learning communities that are focused on the success of all students can be realized.

Imagine...

Imagine each teacher starting the school year with historical data about each student in her or his class. This information could include student achievement results from each student's initial enrollment in school, and would track the student's progress through subsequent years. Now imagine those teachers setting end-of-year goals and measuring their progress toward these goals several times during the year for each student, using assessment tools that the school and district have chosen. By revisiting and measuring their goals throughout the year, teachers are better able to decide whether they need to alter what they are doing to ensure that they reach those year-end goals with their students, and, when ready, teachers can print report cards to send home at the same time the class grades are sent electronically on to the district office.

Imagine students accessing a special password-driven part of the classroom database to add self-assessment data, goals for improvement, and to view assessments and grades. Just imagine students' delight with parents' ability to view or receive, on demand, progress reports about their son and daughter!

Imagine further a school information system that allows teachers to access historical achievement data along with data from each student's emergency card, attendance, record, and other useful information. Collectively, these data could be used to help teachers and administrators positively answer the following questions:

- Are school staffs accomplishing their vision, mission, and purpose?
- Do students know what is expected of them and are they able to deliver it?
- What are students' levels of knowledge and ability?
- Are the instructional practices and/or programs being used with students accomplishing their intent?
- Are the programs being offered cost-effective?

- Is there a continuum of learning that is apparent for all students?
- Are there early indicators of potential failure that teachers can identify, thus giving them the opportunity for interventions to assure all students' success?
- Is there knowledge of all students' academic success?
- Are parents being communicated with effectively concerning student progress and needs?

At the district level, imagine administrators who know the impact of schools' efforts on behalf of students and who use data to show where and when they need to provide new programs, professional development, technical assistance, and funds to achieve the purpose and mission of the district. These administrators could ensure that a continuum of learning is maintained within schools.

Now imagine that all of this information, which helps teachers, schools, and districts perform most effectively for each student, also satisfies all the state and federal departments of education data requirements. Imagine the ability to electronically report to the state and federal agencies with the touch of a key.

Databases are Important to School Improvement

If personnel in districts, schools, and classrooms had access to quality data when they need them and knew how to use them, the world of education could look very different from the way it looks today. Dollars could be spent only on effective programs and perhaps students would not fall through the cracks.

Teachers, administrators, regulatory offices, and school districts need data to understand the impact of their work with schools and children. All educators are struggling to understand precisely what data are needed in order to know how well they are doing and what they need to do differently to get the most effective results.

In ideal settings, the school district assigns personnel to assist in creating and maintaining databases that capture the essence of the district's work, the work of its schools, and the impact of this work on their clients—the students. The district uses these databases to retrieve and manipulate the information they need for their work and, equally important, to provide access to their schools and allowing teachers to access and analyze data on their own.

This comprehensive database, used effectively, allows all staff—district and school—to recognize quality processes, revise or reject ineffective practices, prevent failure, and predict key intervention strategies that ensure every student's success.

Databases

Used here, the term *database* refers to a system of complete, retrievable and organized information that is accessible electronically and that can be easily manipulated. Telephone books, encyclopedias, and dictionaries are common databases that are organized alphabetically to make names and addresses, subjects, and words easy to find. These databases allow users to organize, store, and retrieve information. When these databases are accessed electronically, they are even easier to search and reorganize for use.

In addition to organizing, storing, and retrieving information, schools and districts need to manipulate and summarize information. Databases built upon individual student information help us to:

- know who our students are
- understand how the school population changes over time
- realize the impact of processes and programs on our students
- know current levels of performance
- recognize the relative effectiveness of all our programs and offerings
- know if there are processes that need to change in order to maximize students' learning
- understand if the purposes of our school and district are being met
- understand if we are meeting established standards, and, if not, why not (Is it because the standard is unattainable, or because we are not utilizing appropriate processes to reach the standard?)
- identify problems

- identify what needs to change to prevent future failure
- be accountable (at all levels — state, district, building, teacher, community, parent, and student)

In a student-based database, we are trying to quantify the education-relevant life of each student. (See Figure 1.1.) This database would identify who each student is (demographics), what each student has been experiencing with respect to what we are doing to help her/him learn (school processes), what the student is perceiving about the learning environment (perceptions[1]), and what the student knows (student learning).

Figure 1.1

Student Database

Who are these
students?
(Demographics)

What are they
experiencing?
(School Processes)

What are they
perceiving about
the learning
environment?
(Perceptions)

What do they
know?
*(Student Learning
Results)*

---

[1] Although perceptions are not typically a part of the student achievement database (questionnaires are often administered anonymously and, therefore, cannot be linked to the student identification number), student perceptions can be a major indicator of what needs to change to get different results. Formal questionnaire administration may not be necessary—simply talking with student s can give teachers breakthroughs. For example, when grade three teachers at one elementary school wanted to know how to get all students reading on grade level, they read with the students and asked them questions. This helped teachers understand the concepts their students needed to work on. Many times, the students hold the answers—we just do not always ask them.

A student-based database allows us to analyze the achievement and experiences of our students by aggregating and disaggregating points of information based on the characteristics and experiences of our students—in other words, to summarize results for all students (aggregate), and to reorganize the information for different groups of students (disaggregate). This informs us about the impact of our work. Schools need to be clear about who each student is, and what each student has been experiencing and perceiving, in order to understand the achievement results they are getting with respect to what the student needs to know. This type of database could also support school leaders' efforts to create and sustain professional learning communities focused on success for all students. Without the measurement and monitoring of progress via a database, the effectiveness of the work of many districts, schools, and teachers may never be known. Without a database, schools may never know that redirection of their resources could have made a world of difference to a number of options in a student's life. Without a database teachers are hindered from sharing student information with their student's next teachers. Without a database, student success is left to chance and perception.

Barriers to Creating Databases

When we undertake challenges in education, resistance is first encountered, and then reluctance arises as things are tried. Finally, acceptance comes when the things that are tried begin to work. Some of the barriers that districts may be experiencing with respect to creating databases include:

- not having the information they need to thoughtfully choose a database and lack of understanding of the database tools available
- not having personnel available at the school or district level who can take the database on as a project and lack of technical expertise to deal with the myriad of sources of data
- district students are already high (or low) performers and the teachers and administrators do not feel they need another way to tell them what they already know
- thus far, they have gotten by without one

- fear that the necessary hardware and software will be too costly
- lack of a common mission within schools and within a district
- fear that they will find out things that they do not want to know
- misconception that databases are for "hard-core" statistics only

The Purpose of this Book

The purpose of this book is to help educators think through the issues surrounding the creation and uses of databases established to achieve increased student learning. This book will help educators understand:

- why student achievement databases are needed
- how to create or modify a database that will meet their specific needs
- how to modify an existing database to use it for action research
- what resources and commitments are needed to | establish a continuing database program
- how to get "buy-in" for an adoption of a student achievement database solution
- what information is important to retrieve from the database
- how to translate that information into comprehensive school improvement through data analysis

The task of creating a database is tolerable when one knows that the labor-intensive work of designing, implementing, and using a database will result in analyses that lead to school improvement and, ultimately, to enhanced student learning. This book reviews the important steps of designing, selecting, implementing, maintaining, and reporting from databases without the typical technical methodologies found in most database design books. This book does not reference specific software programs for two reasons: 1) without knowing each school's capacity, no one can recommend database solutions; and 2) the field of technology is changing so quickly, the information would be outdated by the time this book is available.

The text is organized into two sections, designing and using databases. Figure 1.2 on the next page illustrates the major concepts within each section and chapter.

Designing

Chapter 2 describes the importance of clarifying the mission or purpose of the database, its goals and objectives, of identifying potential users and uses of the database *before* beginning the design and implementation process. A database *needs analysis tool* is described and provided which will assist with the selection of database solutions.

Chapter 3 discusses what data to include in a database. Suggestions for designing, implementing, and maintaining a database are also provided.

Using

Chapter 4 shows how to transform data into information through data analyses to be used for continuous improvement. This chapter also summarizes different scores and terms used in student achievement analyses.

Chapter 5 describes methods for translating information and analysis into comprehensive schoolwide improvement.

Chapter 6 is about using the information at all levels to improve education for all students. Examples from across the country are included in this chapter.

Summary

Chapter 7 summarizes the highlights and concludes the information presented in this book, and discusses database solutions for schools and school districts.

The *Appendix* is a set of copy-ready Needs Analysis Form masters that will help educators with the design of a database system.

The *Glossary* includes terms used throughout the book and others that educators will encounter as they learn more about databases, data warehouses, and data analyses. While the terms will be defined in the context of the chapters, they will also appear in the glossary.

Figure 1.2

Steps in Designing and Using a Database

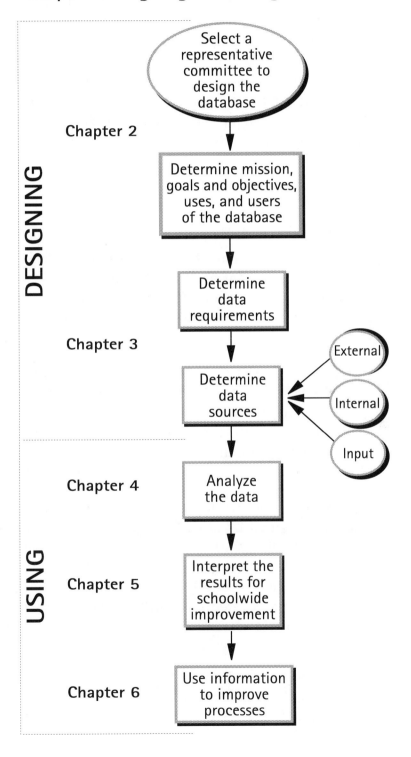

Throughout these chapters are examples from Challenge Unified School District (USD). Although Challenge USD was made up for this publication, the facts are real for many school districts. These examples are included to stimulate thinking about your own situation, not to be copied or taken literally, because they may not meet your specific needs completely. There are many approaches to designing, implementing, and maintaining a database. The intent of this publication is to provide general guidance, not rules, with regard to designing databases and to stimulate thinking about the purpose and use of databases for school improvement. Further, by utilizing the steps outlined in the Database Needs Analysis Form, you will be well prepared to work with either a within-district or commercial database design expert.

Summary

A student achievement database can help teachers, principals, and school district administrators ensure a continuum of learning from school to feeder school. It could also provide valuable information with respect to the effectiveness of teachers, professional development, and specific programs and processes, districtwide, and at each school.

This same database can be accessed from an Internet system for use by district schools to monitor a continuum of learning across grade levels in alignment with the school vision, and to identify specific school needs. Over time, the database would allow school personnel to predict potential successes as well as potential failures and to intercede to prevent failure from occurring and to ensure successes.

Accessed for classroom use, teachers can know exactly how a student has performed on different student achievement measures and standards when the student arrives, monitor each student's progress on an ongoing basis, and know exactly the level attained by each student as he or she leaves for the next grade. Based on data, instructional strategies could be adjusted at any time to ensure attainment of the standards.

Without the use of data at each of these levels, instructional decisions, which ultimately impact students, are based on best guesses, gut feelings, and hunches. Without the use of data that reflect actual learning measures and not just test scores, personnel at each of these levels are probably doing the same things over and over and expecting different results. The point here is that with data we might be able to understand more, understand it differently, and tailor better learning experiences for individual students. *Using data requires databases.*

2

DEFINING THE SCOPE

Efficiency is doing the thing right.
Effectiveness is doing the right thing...
Why bother doing it right if we're
not sure we're doing the right thing?

Peter Drucker
Managing in Turbulent Times

When districts and schools get to the point of knowing they need a database for school improvement, they are often in "emergency" mode and want to buy software, and begin inputting data. This short-term gain can be lost without performing the proper groundwork. These districts and schools often find themselves needing to start over because they didn't begin with a comprehensive plan. Personnel become very frustrated. Although there are a variety of software packages available for district databases, the design and implementation of an effective database requires careful planning, and the utilization of database experts. Further, there must be careful consideration of end uses and users. A thorough analysis of your database needs should be completed before purchasing any software application or contracting for database services.

Three school district examples are shown on the following pages to illustrate the frustrations many school personnel experience when careful planning is not conducted.

Example #1: Five years ago, Ocean Unified School District knew they needed to change their database when external school district reform consultants, working with some of the district's schools, asked for historical student achievement data in digital form. It was only then that the superintendent became aware that only one year of data was available in electronic format and past years were available only in paper format. After further investigation, the superintendent discovered that the current database could only hold data for one year. Each time data were added for a new year, the previous year's data were automatically deleted. Furthermore, demographic data, including student attendance, socioeconomic information, and other data collected and kept by the local County Office of Education were also held in an outdated database system incapable of digital aggregation and disaggregation of data.

The superintendent, new to the district and new to data work, approved the purchase of a new system. A new database program and a dedicated computer were purchased, and the implementation took place without involving the potential users of the database. Unfortunately, this quick fix left the district in an even worse position with respect to data. One year later, the superintendent determined that this database program was a poor choice and did not meet the district or its schools' needs, so they purchased yet another new program and hired someone to manage it.

Sadly, the story goes on and on. It took five years to get a system in place that met their needs. Had they thought through their needs and uses from the beginning, and sought out the advice of a school district database expert, they would have had a cost-effective database and, more important, expedient access to the data they needed.

Example #2: Another Unified School District prided itself on having the biggest and the best of everything. Several years ago, the superintendent of this large district struck what he thought was a fabulous deal with a large database software vendor. The superintendent got Board of Education approval to buy the software and began the implementation phase. Unfortunately, there were several unanticipated costs associated with the software. By the time all the additional costs were uncovered, there was not enough money to support the new system. Therefore, the database remained unfinished indefinitely and investments were lost. Consequently, it took about a decade before staff would overcome their reluctance to decide on another database system that would meet the needs of their schools and district.

Example #3: Little School District determined that they neither had enough money to hire a database consultant nor to purchase a major database product. They set out to create their own "homegrown" database. District technology and research staff spent hours and hours over two years setting up a layout for their database and entering data. Three years later, with not all data entered, they began using the database. Unfortunately the technology department were the only ones who could pull the data out of the database, leaving data unavailable one more time to its schools.

Designing the Database

Designing a database, or thinking through all the issues in order to understand which database solution to commit to, is a time-consuming task, if done well, albeit very worthwhile. Beginning with the end in mind, the following procedure should be considered:

- define the scope of the project
- identify the needs of the potential users of the database
- articulate requirements of people who will be creating and maintaining the database
- determine hardware, financial, and human resource constraints that might affect the database design

Figure 2.1 is a database needs analysis form that can help school districts think through the uses, purposes, and requirements of a database so they can choose an appropriate database solution. Shown in what appears to be a linear process, the thinking through of database needs is really a cyclical process. The cyclical aspect comes into play when many issues become clearer in the ensuing steps and must be revisited more than once. Figure 2.1 is offered as a support in thinking through the issues. A copy-ready master of Figure 2.1 appears in the Appendix (Database Needs Analysis Tool) to help educators think through the design of a database system.

Figure 2.1

Database Needs Analysis Form

❶ ▶ Determine the mission, goals, and objectives of the database.

❷ ▶ Identify who should be on the committee to assist with the design of the database.

❸ ▶ Clarify the role of the committee, including timelines.

❹ ▶ Determine purposes, uses, users, and data requirements.

Figure 2.1 (continued)

Database Needs Analysis Form

⑤▶ Identify the database software that is being used in the district and school

⑥▶ Describe the current networking system.

⑦▶ Describe what the software should do that is not now being done by current practices.

⑧▶ Describe the data that are currently available.

⑨▶ Determine how much has been budgeted for this work.

Figure 2.1 (continued)

Database Needs Analysis Form

10 ▶ Describe the data you want to include in the database.

11 ▶ Select the database design team.

12 ▶ Identify who will input the data.

13 ▶ Identify who will produce the standard reports.

Figure 2.1 (Continued)

Database Needs Analysis Form

⑭ ▶ Identify who will maintain the database.

⑮ ▶ Determine the levels of access, who will have access at each level, and how access will be obtained.

The figures that follow (Figures 2.2 through 2.5) represent the steps required in thinking through database solutions for a district/school. The figures, followed by explanations, are organized by these topics found in the database needs analysis form in Figure 2.1:

- Determine the mission, goals, objective, uses, and users of the database
- Determine what data exists now (in a usable format)
- Determine the desired data
- Determine who is going to do the work
- Determine the levels of access, who will have access at each level, and how access will be obtained

Determine the Mission, Goals, Objectives, Uses, and Users of the Database

Figure 2.2 shows the first steps in designing a database. These steps include determining the mission, getting buy-in, and creating a database system that serves many school and district needs and uses.

The mission is as important to the design, implementation, and maintenance of a database solution as it is for an organization. A mission provides a focus for a project and keeps everyone grounded. A mission needs to be identified by the committee established to design the database, and revisited on an ongoing basis as the database is created. The mission will then need to be revisited when all members of the committee have met and uses and users of the database have been determined. Clear, quantifiable goals and objectives will help the mission become achievable. Goals and objectives will need to be revisited as uses are determined.

Figure 2.2

Determine the Mission, Goals and Objectives, Uses and Users of the Database

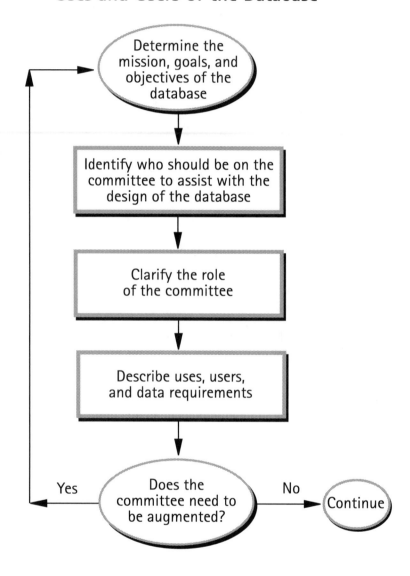

Identify who should be on the committee to assist with the design of the database. As district or school personnel think about selecting a database system for classroom, school, and district improvement, a committee has to be established that is comprised of people with diverse backgrounds and uses for data, including classroom teachers, database designers and programmers, school and district administrators, current data specialists for the district, clerical assistants for data entry, district, county, and/or regional education representatives, school board members, the general public, and other data users. It is important that people in all parts of the organization know that this selection work is going on so anyone with special interests, abilities, or knowledge of existing or desired data can join the committee or provide input into the process. If all appropriate representatives cannot meet, a means of handling collaborative discussions has to be available. To not be all-inclusive, the district runs the risk of seemingly top-down decision-making, or worse, of not considering all district needs, uses and purposes up front. The district also runs the risk of making critical errors because the perceptions and needs of all users were not taken into consideration. The needs of all those currently and potentially involved will be important to the future acceptance and success of the database project.

Clarify the role of the committee, including timelines. Committee members must clearly understand their common mission, role, and timeline for completing this design work. It is essential to document the role of the committee and each member's responsibility, so readers and potential users will understand the context of the final report. The following questions should be considered: Is the committee's role to recommend to another group, or to make an independent decision to purchase and implement a database system? When will the work be done?

Describe purposes, uses, users, and data requirements. List the purposes for creating and using the database. Start with "real" needs. This list will grow as all that is possible is realized; then priorities will have to be assigned. For example: A purpose for a school district database is to provide the school district with information that will help administrators know how each school, grade level, and content area is performing with respect to school district standards, so that additional support may be provided where needed. Other purposes of this same database could be for schools in the district to access information about student achievement to ensure that all students are learning regardless of race, ethnicity, gender; and to provide teachers with historical student achievement data on all their students prior to the beginning of a new school year.

What are the desired uses of the database? Who must have access to the database in order to do their jobs? Who should have access to information to improve the way they are doing their jobs? How will security be maintained with multiple users? Will there be users with minimal software skills and experience? Will database managers be needed? If so, what will be their roles? How will potential users access the database (e.g., computer in classroom, access from home, via the Internet from any computer at any time).

Are there specific data elements required that are related to the desired uses? For example, if one use is to provide analyses to the State Department of Education for categorical programs, are there necessary data to identify, gather, and analyze? Another example would be a grade three teacher querying the database to examine her students' achievement scores on various measures over the past three years. These important considerations will probably uncover new information, or provide additional people to add to the database design committee. (The data to include will be covered in greater depth in Chapter 3.)

Determine What Data Exists Now

Figure 2.3 shows steps in chronicling what data exists in the district and schools, and clarifying what usable data are already available.

Identify the database software that is being used in the district and school offices. In order to understand if a new database program is necessary, database programs currently available and used, and their capabilities, must be analyzed. Find out what is being used, where, and for what purposes. This information will identify what is available and will clarify the level of compatibility between district, school office, and classroom software and hardware. We have seen districts purchase database programs that they expect schools to access, only to find that the schools do not have the hardware or software to connect to the main system. This analysis will also identify whether there is software being used that merely needs to be augmented, or hardware that needs updating. A district must do whatever is reasonably

Figure 2.3

Determine What Data Exists Now

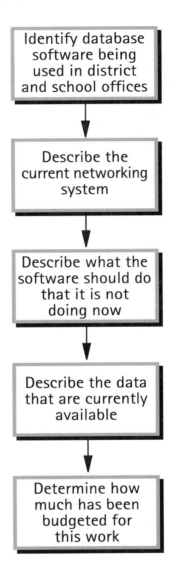

possible to ensure that schools can access and use the district database software, or that if the appropriate software and hardware is not available at the school level, that its purchase is included in the database budget or some other budget.

Describe the current networking system. A comprehensive database solution will require the use of your district and school network. Either your networking will be adequate or your district will need a new networking system. This is a major budgetary consideration, and a key issue in data access, design and implementation. The network drives a good part of the design.

Describe what the software should do that is not now being done by current practices. The responses to this question can be very informative, and will help everyone understand if a new database program is necessary. If the current software program has not been tapped to the extent of its capabilities, it might be that technical support is needed to take full advantage of the current software, or it might be possible that the program needs modification to provide the needed utility. If a database system does not exist, asking this question is another way to get to the uses and purposes of a desired database system.

Describe the data that are currently available. Consider the data that are currently available, their sources and compatibility with different types of hardware and software. What does the district have and in what form? What data do the schools routinely gather? What does your county/regional office have? What can you get from the state database system? What can you get digitally from commercial test vendors or online data agencies? What do the schools share? You may find a wealth of data available that, for some reason or another, was unknown to all potential users. With existing data, a comprehensive database system could be formed. It is important to include what some database engineers call a "data archaeologist" to make sure that existing data are cleaned up and made meaningful and usable. Some superintendents want to have data in the database for everything in the district. This is not always possible, cost-effective, or needed. We need to make sure that the data that are collected and stored for analysis are actually useful for attaining the goals. (See Chapter 4 for elaboration on test score analyses.)

Determine how much has been budgeted for this work. How much is available for database development and maintenance and how much is needed to do it right? If new hardware, software, and networking are required for the schools, make sure these are included in the budget. Database experts tell us that the costs for supporting multiple platforms is truly cost prohibitive for most schools. The cost of supporting two platforms is almost three times the cost of one [1.75(x) + x]. The cost of supporting three becomes exponential x^2. It is extremely important to budget for all of the planning, design, implementation, training, maintenance work and time, and "hidden" costs that will appear.

Determine Desired Data

This piece of the database design requires reflective work about steps already covered:

- ◆ What data are available and how does the district/school want to use the data?
- ◆ What other data are needed?

Describe the data you want to include in the database. Occasionally, when a database system does not deliver the information needed by districts and schools, the fault may not be with the system. It might be an indication that additional data are needed rather than a new software program. However, it must also be a consideration that some data may not be appropriate for some database programs. For instance, districts and schools might earmark questionnaire data as additional data desired. Unfortunately, if a questionnaire was not established with a database in mind, i.e., if the necessary identification was not included on the questionnaire initially, these data will not be linkable to all other records and, therefore, not appropriate for the type of database being used. Questionnaire data most often need to be gathered anonymously so respondents can feel that they can give candid responses. (Refer to the Education for the Future Initiative website, http://eff.csuchico.edu, for information about questionnaire database solutions.)

List all information, demographic, student achievement scores, teacher information, and so on, that needs to be included as part of the data. (Chapter 3 focuses on the data to include in the database.)

Determine Who is Going To Do the Work

Determine who is going to perform the work required in implementing and maintaining a database that will meet its mission. This will be a major budget issue.

Select the database design team. The design of a comprehensive database is an important task and one that requires database expertise. Determine a project manager and involve all the individual(s) who will be responsible for the design and implementation of this database system as early in the process as possible. Sometimes only the software companies per se can modify existing software. It is highly recommended to have a knowledgeable database designer and

Figure 2.4

Determine the Data Desired

Figure 2.5

Determine Who is Going to do the Work

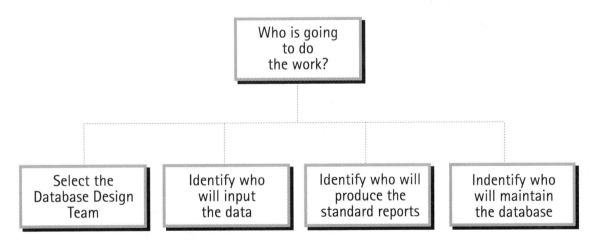

systems programmer, with no commitments to a specific software product, as part of the design committee. Sometimes only the software companies per se can modify the existing software.

The database project manager should be knowledgeable about relational databases (defined in Chapter 3); he/she should know how to program desired reports and queries, and how to work with a variety of school-based data. Database project managers should have a degree in computer science, coursework in statistics, and work experience in education. It is important that the project manager be able to listen to and understand your needs and desired uses of data, and to be able to suggest ways to gather the appropriate data. Chances are you will need a systems programmer who will focus on the operating system and the hardware. Your situation may require an additional network person as well. Data will need some structural work to achieve a comprehensive flow between new and old data and new and old software. A data analyst, also called a data archaeologist, will need to be hired to clean up the data, verify its accuracy and consistency, and to make the data compatible and relatable. Cleansing the data includes: eyeballing the data for duplications and inconsistencies, understanding the data elements to know when an inappropriate number is a keyboard entry problem or some other error, and knowing how to "fix" it.

Identify who will input the data. Data sources will dictate how data get imported or input into the database. For example, if teachers and school administrators desire classroom specific information for use, the committee will need to recommend who will perform the data entry. Consistency, accuracy, security, and confidentiality are important considerations. This question requires reflecting back on the purposes and uses of the database, to the desired data, and the way they will be retrieved. If it is determined that classroom data will be input routinely, the database system will have to allow individuals to input from their classrooms, home, and/or the school office. The database system will need to have input screens created so that the data entry clerks can easily see what information goes where. The database project manager will have to determine how the database will remain accurate, so that individuals inputting in one part of the system cannot change other parts — either accidentally or intentionally.

Identify who will produce the standard reports. Who will be responsible for producing the standard reports? What do you want the standard reports to look like? What about the production of additional reports? Some reports will depend on the human resources available at the district and school levels, with budget implications. A data distribution strategy is necessary.

Querying, the art of questioning the database to produce reports, was once the hardest part of the whole database equation. Now OLAP (online analytical processing) cube browsers (a user interface for browsing data that is stored in an OLAP cube or multidimensional representations of relational data) are available that allow ad hoc querying without programming. Anyone setting up queries must intimately know everything about the database.

Identify who will maintain the database. Just like hardware and software, someone needs to be in charge of the maintenance and security of the database system. This individual needs to have database expertise and familiarity with the district's data, the schools' needs, and overall reporting needs. It is possible that routine maintenance may take place during off-school periods with database experts, or a database specialist may be employed full-time to continuously oversee and maintain the system.

Determine the Levels of Access, Who Will Have Access at Each Level, and How Access Will be Obtained

Once the data to include in the database and the standard reports have been determined, a plan of action for communicating information learned from the data will need to be established. Determine who will need the database information and how they can get it. This is of major importance to the final selection of the database solution. Security is also a major consideration with access. The mission will drive this piece.

Example District

Challenge School District Needs Analysis

Challenge School District wanted a new database system so that teachers could begin to conduct action research; they were truly interested in district and school improvement. The district data office was getting more requests for data analysis than they could fill. There was no way the current system could support the teacher action research project. Additionally, there was a feeling among school personnel that the district was not fulfilling the school's data needs. They wanted to become more proactive about their data analysis work and less reactive to demands and requirements. School personnel wanted a system that effortlessly provides routine information and data analyses on demand, so that they could continuously improve their services to students. A committee was formed to conduct an analysis of their database needs. Their findings are reported below and on the pages that follow.

> Challenge School District is located in Ideal, California. Approximately 10,000 students are enrolled in the district. Challenge School District is comprised of 15 schools—eight elementary, three middle, two comprehensive high, and two alternative high schools. The district committee conducted the analysis of their database needs using the Database Needs Analysis Form shown previously in Figure 2.1. A summary of the results and discussion follow as shown in Figure 2.6.

Figure 2.6

Challenge School District
Database Needs Analysis Form

① Determine the mission, goals, and objectives of the database.

The mission of the resulting database is to support district and school goals to improve student learning by generating information for analysis in user-friendly formats to promote continuous improvement.

The goals of the database are to:

Goal 1: Understand student achievement needs of the district:
Objectives:
(a) To analyze student achievement data by grade level and understand where student achievement is lowest
(b) To recognize where and when interventions are required across the district and within schools

Goal 2: Understand the needs of the teachers with respect to standards across the district:
Objectives:
(a) To analyze student achievement data by grade levels, school, and by teacher to learn which teachers need support and in what areas
(b) To recognize where and when interventions are required across the district and within schools

Goal 3: Predict potential failure:
Objectives:
(a) To review historical data to identify trends relating to student failure
(b) To apply learning of past performance to current students and intervene to prevent failure

Goal 4: Provide the ability to supply expedient and accurate reports to state and federal agencies:
Objectives:
(a) To provide all concerned instant access to desired information, without dependence on other entities,
(b) To establish state and federal reports (standard reports) with a push of a button

Figure 2.6 (Continued)

Challenge School District
Database Needs Analysis Form

 Identify who should be on the committee to assist with the design of the database.
It was determined that the following people will be needed on the committee to select a database for the district:

From the district—
    Representatives of the:
- Assistant Superintendent for Educational Services
- Assistant Superintendent for Fiscal Management
- Attendance Officer
- Curriculum Director
- Evaluation and Research Office
- Information and Management Services
- Categorical Programs/Grants/Special Projects
- Staff Development Coordinator
- Clerical Assistants (for database input)
- Database Specialist

From the schools—
- The Principals
- Classroom Teacher Representatives
- School Secretaries (who assist with the data)
- Technology Specialists
- Students

From the County Office of Education—
- Directors of Curriculum and Instruction
- Directors of Information Services

Others—
- Database Consultant
- School Board Members
- Parent/Community Representatives

 Clarify the role of the committee, including timelines.
The purpose of this committee is to:
- review the current database system and structure
- clarify uses and desires for data
- identify desired data
- recommend a system that will give the data needed to perform significant data analyses

The final recommendation of the committee will be presented in writing to all schools and the district office for review. Comments will be incorporated and, provided that the ultimate recommendation is not changed, the needs analysis will be presented to the Board of Education at their January meeting. Upon their approval, the committee's recommendation will be implemented. The work of the committee will be completed by November.

Figure 2.6 (Continued)

Challenge School District
Database Needs Analysis Form

 Describe purposes, uses, users, and data requirements.

The desired database will be multipurposed. Challenge School District wants a database that will enable personnel to analyze student performance results in order to understand their impact on student learning (i.e., instruction, professional development, school improvement models, the schools, and the teachers). They want to pinpoint—from the data—what needs to change that will lead to the continuous improvement of the performance of their jobs. They also want all users to be able to create their own special and specific data reports.

Challenge School District's data will be created, maintained, and warehoused in the district office. The district will retrieve and use data for its purposes and will make data accessible online to the schools for school purposes. Teachers will add to the database and access the database for their action research work. The intent of the resulting data analysis work, to be conducted via this database, is to understand how the district, schools, and teachers can continuously improve so that all students can and will learn.

The committee developed a matrix of uses for data (see Table 2.1 on the following pages) and attempted to make a comprehensive list of the data required for these uses. They realized that sometimes aggregated (group) information would be required and at other times student records organized by attributes—such as ethnicity and gender—would be required for disaggregated analyses. It was clear to the committee that no matter which analyses are desired, individual student information must remain linked to student identifiers for accurate reporting—exactly why a database is needed. (Details will be discussed in Chapter 4.) They also understood that they could not meet all objectives if they did not link student identifiers to school identifiers as well.

Table 2.1

Challenge School District
Uses and Data Requirements

Document in Progress

	Multiple Measures	Disaggregation	Questionnaires	Demographics	Student Achievement
The School Portfolio	Four years, all grade levels in reading and math on NRT, and non-NRT for each subject area.	By program—Title 1, Migrant redesignated FED, LEP-content, LEP-ELD, special Ed, plus disaggregated by gender and ethnicity.	Not required, but strongly recommended.	40% Free and Reduced Lunch or 40% ELL.	7 NCEs growth.
Achieving Schools An award application	All grade levels—reading and math. Determine how many do not meet, meet, or exceed standards based on at least two of: NRT, teacher-assigned grades or other measures (i.e., writing samples).	By program—Title 1, Migrant, redesignated FEP, LEP-content, LEP-ELD, Special Ed (evaluated on standards), plus disaggregated by gender and ethnicity.	Do not require, but think it is a good idea.	Yes—must have 50 percent AFDC.	NRT gain of 3 NCEs in at least reading/language arts and math.
AVID Advancement via individual determination	To determine that there are students with college potential not currently on the college track.	The target population must be underserved minorities.	Parent, teacher, and student.	School must have underserved minority population.	Students are identified as follows: passing non-college track courses, have college potential.
Blue Ribbon	Sustained high achievement in reading/math on NRT CRT, Alternative Assessments.	By demographics if more than 15% of school's population (i.e., language proficiency, ethnicity, socioeconomic status.	Not required, but strongly recommended.	Enrollment, Attendance (student and teacher), discipline, ethnicity, program participation, language, language proficiency, socioeconomic status.	At or above 57 NCE for all students (or majority of students) for 5 years and/or 7 NCEs growth for minority students (15% of population).

Table 2.1 (Continued)

Challenge School District
Uses and Data Requirements

Document in Progress

	Multiple Measures	Disaggregation	Questionnaires	Demographics	Student Achievement
Coordinated Compliance Review (CCR)	All grade levels—reading and math. Determine how many do not meet, meet, or exceed standards based on at least two of: NRT, teacher-assigned grades or other measures (i.e., writing samples).	By program—Title 1, Migrant, redesignated FEP, LEP-content, LEP-ELD, Special Ed (evaluated on standards), plus disaggregated by gender and ethnicity.	None required.	The Consolidated Programs and Information Management Department of the CDE maintains demographic data on all schools in the state and uses it for many purposes, including identifying schools to receive CCR team visits.	Multiple measures are required.
Curriculum Audit A voluntary process that districts can purchase, offered by a joint venture between ACSA, CCSESA, and Fenwick English's Curriculum Audit Group	Standard 4 requires that data be collected from a variety of sources, and for a variety of purposes.	Equity is one of the five standards.	As part of examining the assessment system, it is recommended that surveys be used to give staff and leadership a distinct picture of how well the district's mission is being accomplished. Their surveys include questions like: • This semester, how many of your teachers usually return corrected papers within two days? • This semester, how many of your teachers explained their grading system? • Can you read well enough to do the work in your courses? • How much homework is assigned? Of that, how much do you do?	Total profile of all sites in district, over time.	Audit standards specify that systems exist to collect data for several purposes to: • inform instruction in the classroom • determine effectiveness of programs at the site • determine effectiveness of programs at the district level • determine effectiveness and equity in delivery of instruction throughout the district A key focus is to ensure that what is tested matches what is taught.

Table 2.1 (Continued)

Challenge School District
Uses and Data Requirements

Document in Progress

	Multiple Measures	Disaggregation	Questionnaires	Demographics	Student Achievement
Distinguished Schools An award application	Adds points—but not required.	No.	No.	Yes.	Yes—Schools can submit what they like.
Grant Writing	Better chance of getting funded.	Better chance of getting funded.	Better chance of getting funded.	Better chance of getting funded.	Better chance of getting funded.
Healthy Start A competitive grant process	Of student, family, and community risk factors.	Applications are strengthened by disaggregation of data regarding health/safety risks, as well as achievement.	Successful applications typically include extensive input from the community regarding needs that affect health/safety and schooling.	High-poverty, multi-ethnic schools have priority for funding.	Data about student achievement strengthen the application. Healthy Start's intent is to increase readiness to learn.
Learning Results IPI 4 Submitted with self-review	All grade levels—reading and math. Determine how many do not meet, meet, or exceed standards based on at least two of: NRT, teacher-assigned grades or other measures (i.e., writing samples).	By program—Title 1, Migrant, redesignated FEP, LEP-content, LEP-ELD, Special Ed (evaluated on standards).	No.	Provided by state.	Does not meet, meets, or exceeds local standards as measured by multiple measures.
Local Improvement Plan (LIP) Must be submitted by districts receiving categorical funds	Required.	Gender, ethnicity, SES, special education, language proficiency.	The school community is supposed to be involved in formulating the plan—but *how* is left up to the locals.	Yes.	The LIP describes how data will be collected (what measures) and how they will be used (reporting to parents and to governance committees).
Program Quality Review (PQR)	Yes. Typically, the measures are classroom-based and not shared across the school or over time.	Yes. Schools are asked to look at student work or representative samples of student work from significant subpopulations—including LEP and GATE.	No. Not required, although a school could use them as part of its self-review.	No.	Yes. In a soft, locally defined manner focused on one subject, with the option to consider only representative samples of student work.

Table 2.1 (Continued)

Challenge School District
Uses and Data Requirements

Document in Progress

	Multiple Measures	Disaggregation	Questionnaires	Demographics	Student Achievement
Safe and Drug-Free Schools • An entitlement • Description of program included in LIP	No.	No.	Or some way to assess local situation regarding drugs and violence.	No.	No.
School Accountability Report Card A document schools are required to publish yearly	Not required.	Not required.	Not required.	Enrollment, average daily attendance, ethnic and LEP breakdowns.	At the minimum, standardized test results and goals are required.
Title I Schoolwide	Yes. As chosen by district. Site can collect additional data as desired.	Yes. By gender, ethnicity, socioeconomic status, language proficiency, and disability.	A complete needs analysis is required. The attitudes and opinions portion of it could be obtained through discussion groups or through surveys.	Yes. School must have children with at least 40 percent free and reduced lunch.	Yes.
Title I Targeted Assistance	Yes. As chosen by district. Site can collect additional data as desired.	Yes. By gender, ethnicity, socioeconomic status, language proficiency, and disability.	No, but parent involvement is required—and surveys are one way to involve them.	No.	Yes. Student achievement data must be based on multiple measures in language arts and mathematics.
Title VII	Yes.	LEP/ Non-LEP/ School Climate.	Yes.	Yes.	English proficiency, native language proficiency, valid and reliable instrument.

Table 2.1 (Continued)

Challenge School District
Uses and Data Requirements

Document in Progress

	Multiple Measures	Disaggregation	Questionnaires	Demographics	Student Achievement
TUPE An entitlement for tobacco use prevention based on application which describes current levels of risk/use and plans to reduce risk/use	No.	You are asked to collect data about tobacco use and your effectiveness in reducing it for three categories of students: those already smoking, those in high-risk groups, and the general population.	To determine current incidence, to set goals for reduction.	No, except as needed to isolate high-risk groups—girls, children of smokers, etc.	No.
Western Association of Schools and Colleges (WASC) A joint process—accreditation for high schools by a private agency and the state's program quality review process	Yes. The school is asked to gather data from many sources to complete its self-study, including SAT, ACT, and other standardized test scores, grades, performance assessments, and data about the success of graduates.	Yes. General direction is given to the effect that the school should consider significant subgroups in analyzing data.	Or some way to get attitudinal data, like *Voices From the Inside*, or discussion groups.	Yes. A full description of the school is included in the self-study.	Variety of assessment strategies to evaluate students and drive school program development.

The committee determined that there would be multiple users of the database at the district, school, and classroom levels. Not all users will be accessing the same parts of the database at the same time, but they need to be able to, if necessary. While the community may ultimately be users of the data, the committee did not feel it should have access to the database—at least at this time. Potential users include the following:

District level—
  Curriculum Office
  Fiscal Office
  School Improvement Office
  Categorical Programs Office
  Professional Development Committee
  Evaluation and Research Office
  Superintendent
  Grant-writing Office
  Professional Development Committee

School level—
  Principal
  Attendance clerks
  Teachers
  Support Staff
  School Psychologist
  Resource Teachers
  Speech Teacher
  Reading Recovery Teachers

Classroom level—
  Teachers
  Teacher Assistants
  Students (i.e., own record only)

Community level—
  Parents
  Community

Figure 2.6 (Continued)

Challenge School District
Database Needs Analysis Form

 Identify the database software that is being used in the district and school offices.
Currently, the Challenge Unified School District holds student information in several different database software packages that do not allow schools access online or through the network. Some of the packages are incompatible with other hardware and software programs that the schools are using. In the past year, the district has allowed schools to download their data. Unfortunately, schools have found errors in the data, and then have had to update district files as well as their own. The schools use different commercial software at the elementary and secondary school levels to track student enrollment, attendance, and course data. Individual teachers and program offices have selected their own software to track what little program data they do track, such as Reading Recovery, Title I, and/or Special Education student performance, so there is no consistency across, or even within, schools. The district does not have a chosen or recommended hardware platform so all platforms exist throughout the district.

 Describe the current networking system.
Challenge Unified School District is in the process of upgrading its district server and linking all schools and classrooms with high-speed data transfer lines.

 Describe what the software should do that is not now being done by current practices.

The district would like data to be available and user-friendly to anyone who needs to use them. They would like the data to be easy to access, manipulate, analyze, and chart.

Schools agree, and in addition, they want data to help them see the big picture of education at the school, e.g., historical student achievement cohort charts, disaggregated by demographics, school processes, and teacher. At the classroom level, the schools want teachers to access student data from a historical achievement perspective, to track performance for every student to the objective level on standardized tests and local assessments. Teachers will need to aggregate and disaggregate information. Teachers also need a way to enter their own assessment data for their action research either in an ongoing fashion or from a school or classroom database.

Figure 2.6 (Continued)

Challenge School District
Database Needs Analysis Form

 Describe the data that are currently available.

At the school level, for each student, the school and district has student name and identification number, prior schools attended, when they were there and length of time, ethnicity, grade level, date(s) of enrollment, emergency information, health records, attendance, and the federal and state programs for which the student qualifies and in which the student participates. Teachers have authentic assessment rubrics and grades for each student, but mostly on paper.

At the district level, for each student, the school and district have student name and identification number. The district receives ethnicity, grade-level information, date(s) of enrollment, and state and federal program information from the schools. Additionally, the district database includes competency test results, high school course information, and degree to which graduation requirements are being met. In a different database, for each year taken, the school and district also have standardized achievement total test scores and subtest scores. At the district level, data are recorded on how the students performed on standardized tests, disaggregated by ethnicity, language fluency, grade level, and by school.

From test publishers, the school and district can get individual student raw scores, standard scores, stanines, percentiles, and Normal Curve Equivalents (NCEs) in digital form that include some demographics.

 Determine how much has been budgeted for this work.

Enough has been budgeted to do everything the committee determines needs to be done. We know there will be great up-front costs, and hope that the ongoing costs will be reasonable. We know we must budget for unforeseen costs. The Board of Education believes this investment will ultimately pay off in saved time and energy, and will produce analyses that will help everyone know how to work smarter and not harder. We have spent hundreds of thousands of dollars to get mediocre data in the past in a less than timely manner. We want to do it right this time.

 Describe the data you want to include in the database.

At the school level, the database should include data on student achievement, over time, for each student, including authentic assessments and teacher grades. At the school and classroom levels, the committee would like the capability to link questionnaire responses by grade level as opposed to individuals. The committee would also like to have school and classroom level reports of how students perform with respect to district standards. Teachers would like to start each new year with the historical data on each student on their roster, and use ongoing assessments to ensure student attainment of all standards.

Figure 2.6 (Continued)

Challenge School District
Database Needs Analysis Form

 Select the database design team.

This committee recommends hiring a database project manager who could become familiar with what we have, who can help choose a database solution, and who has no vested interest in any of the decisions of the committee. The project manager will work with district staff to design the database around the information provided in this needs analysis, and a comprehensive list of the desired data, analyses, and reports. Budget and initial work will determine if the manager can be hired as an employee, or if she/he will train at least two of our current staff members to maintain the database system. Our current preference is the latter.

We will seek the assistance and advice of the database consultant and software company to locate knowledgeable systems programmers and other database engineers.

 Identify who will input the data.

At the district level, the Information and Management Office will be responsible for entering data. First the database manager will import or download those data that already exist in digital form into one location. Data entry clerks will input information that needs to be added at the school level. Teachers will enter student grades, performance and content assessment measures, and any other appropriate classroom-specific data.

 Identify who will produce the standard reports.

This committee recommends that district staff work closely with the database consultant to establish standard routine reports, as well as specialized reports. The Information and Management Office will be responsible for providing individuals who do not have a vested interest in the data results to generate routine and specialized reports. District staff and teachers will be able to produce their own reports with training and technical assistance from the district office. Special request reports that are not automatically available to the schools and program officers can be requested via e-mail from the Information and Management Office. All these reports should be online reports that are accessible to school sites. The schools, in turn, can choose to use the information online or print them out.

There will be three types of reports available to users with specific needs:
- Standard Reports, for—
   Schools
   Teachers
   District
- Specialized Reports
   e.g., Special Education Office, Title 1
- Special Request Reports
   These are the types of reports for which this new system is being built. End users need to be able to produce their own reports.

Figure 2.6 (Continued)

Challenge School District
Database Needs Analysis Form

 Identify who will maintain the database.

The Head of Information and Management Services will be responsible for the database and its maintenance. Off-school periods will be set aside to conduct major database maintenance, when the system is unavailable to users. This person will also be responsible for training staff members to use the database.

Determine the levels of access, who will have access at each level, and how access will be obtained.

Major historical district data will be warehoused at the district office. School personnel will be able to access the database online by password whenever they need to, and will be able to add specified information to the database, such as classroom level assessments and attendance at specified times. Beyond these times, the data warehouse will be "read only". Security issues will need to be put into place to ensure that no alterations in the data take place and to enable everyone to use desired parts of the database.

Summary

Selecting a database solution for districts and schools to use for school improvement is a detail-oriented task. Before any selections can take place, the mission of the database, its goals and objectives, end users, and uses must be very carefully identified. Conducting a comprehensive needs analysis involving the potential end users and people with database expertise is a necessary and excellent way to begin the journey.

3

READYING DATA
FOR THE DATABASE

Every school district needs a "digital nervous system" that would help educators manage their schools more efficiently and serve students better.

Bill Gates
Chairman and CEO
Microsoft Corporation

Now that the needs for a comprehensive database system have been analyzed, it is necessary to put the data and data requirements together in a form that will enable the creation of the database and, eventually the data analyses that will meet the ultimate purposes and uses. Remember that the purpose of this book is to help "laypersons" understand what is entailed in designing and using a comprehensive database. A database professional will be required to actually put these many details together into a useful form. Hopefully with the help of this chapter, you will be able to understand what that professional needs to do and to lend assistance.

This chapter focuses on readying the data for the database, which includes defining the terms, identifying the data desired in the database, and documenting the data specifications.

Focus the Database

The building of a database management system (DBMS) needs to focus on the database needs analysis and the desired end analyses. The most crucial pieces of information from the database needs analysis related to data studied in Chapter 2 are:

- Mission, goals and objectives
- Purposes and uses
- Users
- Data requirements
- Data on hand
- Desired data

Let us use Challenge Unified School District's database needs analysis as an example: The mission of the resulting database is to support district and school goals to improve student learning by generating information for analysis in user-friendly formats to promote continuous improvement. The purposes are basically for continuous improvement at three levels: district, school, and classroom. The database needs analysis committee determined there would be standard reports, special reports for categorical programs and such, and ongoing access by classroom teachers and administrators throughout the district. At times, the district would need to access the majority of data, but most of the time, people would need only portions of the database. Some of the district needs would require gathering large amounts of data that will not often be used. (We are dealing here with a student achievement database. Attendance, accounting, grade reports, etc., are dealt with in other ongoing databases, that we hope to be able to use together.)

What Data?

Provided their database consultant agrees, Challenge Unified School District will probably set up a comprehensive data warehouse that will allow them to make informative analyses at the district, school, and classroom levels. The data in the data warehouse will be accessed by the end users. The Challenge committee must think about what data they want in their database, and not have it become a data dumping ground. The larger the database, the slower the analyses, and the harder it is to maintain, clean and understand.

The database committee reviewed resources on education-related data analyses they would want to perform that include those they now perform and those they might want to perform in the future (data analyses are discussed in Chapter 4). They determined that they could perform any analyses by gathering data around the four categories of data as described in *Data Analysis for Comprehensive Schoolwide Improvement* (Bernhardt, 1998, page 15) and shown on the next page in Figure 3.1. The four categories include demographics, student learning, school processes, and perceptions data. (Notice the similarities to Figure 1.1, Chapter 1.) What Figure 3.1 also shows is the interactions, or crossing of data, which will be done in the analysis phase.

It did seem that these data could possibly cover all the uses and purposes expressed in the database needs analysis. So using the four categories as organizers, the committee listed the possible data Challenge Unified School District would want to gather, (Table 5.1), and compared that list to the identified uses and purposes. The committee soon realized that there were demographics that they wanted for individual students, and others that they wanted at the school and the district levels (some of which could be calculated data from individual student demographics—in other words, aggregate data). It also became clear that, as a committee, they could clarify what data they wanted in the database and why. The educational administrative staff would have to help clarify the number of years to go back, the other data elements, and what they usually look like. It was also clear that the actual attribute and specification design had to be left up to the technical staff, since they know how databases work. The committee and the technical staff knew that it would not be long before they would run into difficulties, without professional help.

Figure 3.1

Multiple Measures of Data

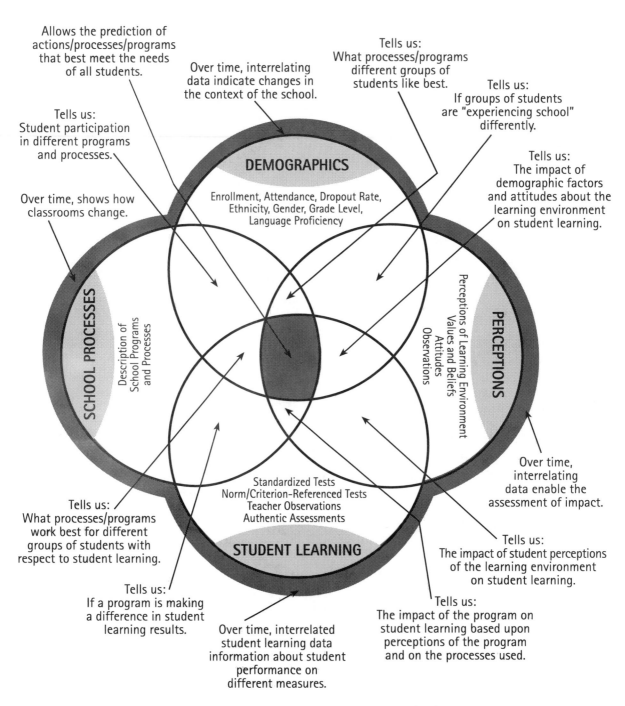

Allows the prediction of actions/processes/programs that best meet the needs of all students.

Tells us: Student participation in different programs and processes.

Over time, shows how classrooms change.

Over time, interrelating data indicate changes in the context of the school.

Tells us: What processes/programs different groups of students like best.

Tells us: If groups of students are "experiencing school" differently.

Tells us: The impact of demographic factors and attitudes about the learning environment on student learning.

DEMOGRAPHICS

Enrollment, Attendance, Dropout Rate, Ethnicity, Gender, Grade Level, Language Proficiency

SCHOOL PROCESSES

Description of School Programs and Processes

PERCEPTIONS

Perceptions of Learning Environment Values and Beliefs Attitudes Observations

Standardized Tests
Norm/Criterion-Referenced Tests
Teacher Observations
Authentic Assessments

STUDENT LEARNING

Over time, interrelating data enable the assessment of impact.

Tells us: The impact of student perceptions of the learning environment on student learning.

Tells us: What processes/programs work best for different groups of students with respect to student learning.

Tells us: If a program is making a difference in student learning results.

Over time, interrelated student learning data information about student performance on different measures.

Tells us: The impact of the program on student learning based upon perceptions of the program and on the processes used.

Source: From *Data Analysis for Comprehensive Schoolwide Improvement* (p.15), by Victoria L. Bernhardt, 1998, Larchmont, NY: Eye on Education. Copyright © 1998 Eye on Education, Inc. Reprinted with permission.

Data Elements

The data that Challenge Unified School District wanted in their database are shown below by demographics, student learning, school processes, and perceptions.

Demographics

Demographics are the statistical characteristics of human populations—who are the students, teachers, and other staff members in the school or school district. Demographics help build the current and historical context of the school and school district, while providing data for predicting future situations. Used with student achievement results, schools are able to verify if all groups of students are achieving. Demographics used with perceptions help the school district pinpoint where the differences in perceptions of the learning environment lie and give hints on how to improve both the perceptions and the learning environment. Used with school processes, demographics can ensure that every student is receiving equal opportunities to learn.

Demographics are most often used to disaggregate group data. As shown in Table 3.1 on the next page, disaggregation is the separating out of different groups by another variable to understand differences and similarities, usually by one or more demographic variable, such as gender and/or ethnicity. For example, schools often want to know if there are student learning differences for boys and girls, so they disaggregate student achievement scores by gender.

Table 3.1

Demographics

Student Demographics	Staff Demographics	School Demographics
Identification number	Identification number	The aggregate of everything that would be collected for the students
Social security number	Social security number	Enrollment projections
Name (last, first, middle)	Name (last, first, middle)	Birth rates for previous years
Address	Address	School safety incidents
Gender	Gender	Crime rate
Ethnicity	Ethnicity	Economic base of the community
Date of birth	Date of birth	Housing trends
Place of birth	Place of birth	Names of administrators
Date of enrollment (could be multiple)	Beginning date (could be multiple)	Names of staff
Date of exit (could be multiple)	Exit date (could be multiple)	Services provided
Number of years in the school	Reason for exit (could be multiple)	Program offerings
Number of years in the district	Number of years in the district	Athletic offerings
Mother's name and address	Current assignment	
Father's name and address	Assignments and dates	
Guardian's name and address	Contact in emergency	**District Demographics**
Contact in emergency	Types of certification and dates	The aggregate of everything that would be collected for the students and staff
Guardian's socioeconomic status	Attendance	The aggregate of everything that would be collected for the schools
Attendance	Tardies	
Tardies	English language fluency	
English language fluency	Salary history	
Language spoken at home	Educational history and dates	
Free and reduced lunch status	Health issues	
Health issues		
Suspensions		
Discipline referrals		
Educational history and dates		
Extracurricular activities		
Special needs		

School Processes

School processes refer to the instructional and assessment strategies used in the school or classroom, program participation, and/or other offerings. This variable is important for understanding the impact of our instructional practices and interventions on student learning. School processes that Challenge Unified School District wanted to track follow:

- Current grade
- Current teacher
- Current advisor
- Interventions (e.g., Reading Recovery, Special Education)
- Program participation (e.g., Adopt-A-Watershed)
- Innovative processes (e.g., multi-ages classroom)
- Calendar (year-round, traditional)
- Standards
- Curriculum objectives
- Master schedule
- Retention

Student Learning

Student learning refers to measures of student achievement, such as norm-referenced tests, criterion-referenced tests, performance assessments, classroom assessments. Basically these are variables related to our best estimates of students' knowledge.

- Standardized test scores:
  - Raw scores
  - Standard scores
  - NCEs (which are standard scores, normalized)
  - Percentiles
  - Percent correct
- Teacher given grades
- Performance assessments:
  - Rubric scores
- Standards met

Perceptions

Since people's perceptions are their reality, it is important for continuously improving schools to know what their clients are thinking. Questionnaires given regularly are helpful in identifying issues that need to be addressed. Challenge Unified School District will continue to gather student, teacher, and parent questionnaire data anonymously and separate from the student achievement database. The technology specialist will disaggregate the perceptions data by demographics and processes, and provide those results to the teachers. Note that perceptual data often are not part of the database because of its anonymous nature, but may help in guiding a district to continuous improvement.

Existing Data

Challenge School District began implementing their comprehensive database by obtaining data that were available from the district office, school offices, and outside organizations. As their needs analysis stated, they were able to get individual student achievement scores as well as some demographic data from test publishers, which created the skeleton of their existing database. Other information from the existing district and school databases was imported. Information was verified and additional desired data were entered into the database by data entry clerks. When the database is up and running, teachers will enter grades and authentic assessment data for their classes.

Because we want to disaggregate and interact the data in many ways, we need to take care in linking the data to individual students, as illustrated in Figure 3.2.

Figure 3.2

Multiple Measures / Data Elements

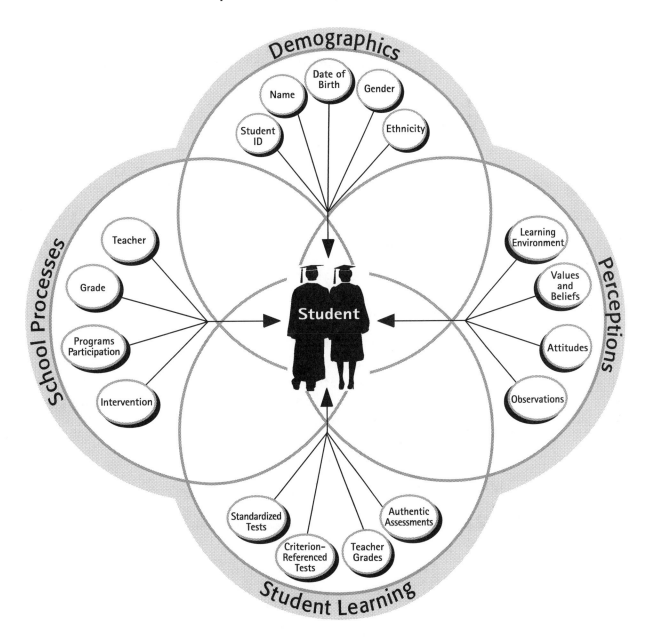

The Design

After each of the necessary data elements were identified, the Challenge database committee and their database designers defined the entities and relationships, attributes, and attribute specifications. (Again, please note, this is but one example. There are many ways this design can be accomplished. There are other terms that can be used as well. Work with your database consultant to agree on terms and definitions.) The terms to be used in this example are defined below.

Entity

Databases are made up of entities which are composed of attributes. An entity (also known as a *record, table,* or *file*) is anything about which you want to track information. Challenge's definition of one entity is each student. Student 1 would have demographic, student learning, school process, and perceptions variables related to her/him. After defining what constitutes an entity in the database, Challenge identified the individual attributes within each entity.

Identify the Attributes

Attributes are characteristics of entities. Attributes (also known as *fields*) in a student achievement database would include, among many others, the elements in the circles of Figure 3.2 (i.e., name, ethnicity, and gender of the student). Table 3.2 offers a simple design for laying out the entities and attributes.

Table 3.2

Attribute Design

	Field 1	Field 2	Field 3	Field 4	Field 5	Field 6	Field 7	Field 8
	Last Name	First Name	Middle Name	ID #	DOB	Gender	Ethnicity 1	Ethnicity 2
Student 1 (Entity 1)								
Student 2 (Entity 2)								
Student 3 (Entity 3)								
Student 4 (Entity 4)								
Student 5 (Entity 5)								

Attribute Specifications

After the attributes have been determined, their characteristics must be specified. This process of attribute specification is the next step in the entity structure definition process. Attribute specifications control the kind of information that can be entered into the attribute. Attribute specifications would include the attribute name (e.g., student identification number, student last name, student first name) and data type (e.g., text, number, date/time, yes/no) for each attribute in an entity, as well as their properties. Properties include attribute size, format, decimal places, default value, etc., depending on the software program. The educational experts need to specify what data they want, what form the data should be in, and what they want out of the database. Database designers will determine the types of attributes that will generate the desired data. This is an important step for clarification and accuracy. Table 3.3 on page 58 shows examples of attribute specifications.

Table 3.3

Example Attribute Specifications

Field Name	Data Type	Description
Student ID	Number	Identification number assigned by district
Last Name	Text	Proper name
First Name	Text	Proper name
Middle Initial	Text	Middle initial
Birthdate	Date	Month/Day/Year of birth
Gender	Text	M or F (male or female)
Ethnicity 1	Text	First choice
Ethnicity 2	Text	Second choice
Ethnicity 3	Text	Third choice

Properties of Student ID	
Field size	10 characters
Format	Standard
Validation Rule	No less than 10 characters No greater than 10 characters
Validation Text	Needs ID number
Required	Yes
Allow zero length	No
Default value	Null
Indexed	Yes (no duplicates)

Properties of Middle Initial	
Field size	1 character
Format	Standard
Validation Rule	No more than one
Validation Text	Can be blank
Required	No
Allow zero length	Yes
Default value	Null
Indexed	Yes

Identification Number

The purpose for going through this huge process of both gathering and storing data is to be able to retrieve them in a useful form later. That means we must be able to link together many different pieces of data. A student identification number is required to link each student's test score results from year to year with grades and demographics. A student identification number additionally can establish the structure required to link relational databases to each other. This is one of the hardest parts of building a database. This identification number must be one that does not change, can follow a student from school to school, and is standard enough that anyone entering data would know it, understand it, and not alter it unexpectedly. For example, if letters become a part of an identifier, some data entry clerks might enter the identifier with capital letters, others with small letters, etc., that would lead to multiple entries for the same person. This and the fact they are not unique is why names are not good identifiers. Names can be entered in so many ways—with middle name, middle initial, formal first name, and nickname—that each entry would become a different person. We would like to see schools and school districts use two unique identifiers. Many school districts across the country use social security numbers as one identifier. Schools and school districts gather this information upon student enrollment. It is available. In numerous cases, however, there is some reluctance to use it. This is an issue that can be addressed with the parents. It is possible to use social security numbers, with parent approval. Some database architects recommend using numbers for identifiers that have no meaning with or without social security numbers. Caution would have to be exercised, in case of duplicates.

Documenting the Design

Entity specifications document the attributes and entities in terms of what they are, their format and default value, and how the data get validated. How the attributes and entities fit together in a relational sense also needs to be specified to provide a road map to the data in the database. This includes the source of tables, the meanings of the keys, and the relationships between the tables.

During the design process, it is important to keep a record of your decisions and reasons for making them. This documentation will be invaluable to the overall design and to maintain input consistency and output accuracy.

Any large database will have some data problems because of the hugeness of the task. Some common problems include inconsistent file names, attribute lengths, attribute orders, descriptions, identities, value assignment, and incomplete entries. Some of these potential problems can be avoided and/or easily spotted through careful and detailed specifications and documentation.

Database Coordination

After the database structure has been designed and the database solution installed, the data have to be input into the database. Inputting and importing the data accurately and consistently could be one of the most time-consuming and costly parts of the entire process. The quality of the data that comes out of the database is dependent upon the quality of data that is put into the database. This is where the role of the data archaeologist is crucial.

Different ways to get data into the database include:
- direct keyboard entry
- screen-oriented database software (e.g., touch screen)
- another software package that will interface with the database
- importing from another database
- optical character recognition (OCR) that gets converted to numbers through a scanning machine

As a tip, always start with importing existing data from another database, if available. Any existing database will need to be "cleaned up" to flow with the other data.

Quality Control

Maintaining a high-quality database requires time and effort. Database quality is assured through:

- capturing data as close to the source as possible
- careful data gathering and importing procedures
- consistent use of each attribute
- care in the creation of the attributes, error checking at input
- ongoing proofreading
- provisions for corrections

It is important to make decisions about standardizing input early in the design process. Standardizations need to be made in the way data are entered, the attributes, whether or not any items are italicized, capitalized, or boldfaced, if there are lists to be bulleted or numbered, and when the database will be backed up. Whenever possible, use forced choice options (such as pulldown menus, *yes/no* options) rather than typing in data in order to avoid unintended variation. Failure to standardize the way names will be treated, for instance, can cause major errors in analyses later on. For example, those responsible for the database must decide if proper names are going to be put in the database rather than informal names (e.g., Victoria or Vickie), or if the middle initial or middle name will be included. When it comes to querying, ultimately looking for Vickie L. may never lead to Victoria or even Vickie. Each of these names could be perceived as different entities, i.e., different people. The rationale and importance of the standardization must be communicated to everyone. The use of student identification numbers will help this matter considerably.

The order of the attributes may be dictated by the nature of the information. In many cases, there are options, more than one of which might be reasonable. The sequence should be logical, useful, and convenient for the user. A sequence that works well for data entry personnel may not work as well for the database user. Another consideration is the ease with which data can be rearranged. It should be possible to rearrange or sort data, either at entry or output, so that data entry needs and end user needs can both be met. Again, it is important to document how the database is set up and how data are to be entered so that anyone new to the database system can use it successfully.

Input screens are very important for accurate data inputting. Some database management systems allow for the development of scannable forms for data entry with a computer screen that looks like the hard copy. Most database architects will work with the education representatives to create input screens that will make data entry easy, accurate, and time-efficient. Large databases have different screens. Organization has to be thoughtful to avoid time wasted moving between screens.

Data with Meaning

Make sure meaningful data are being entered. For instance, raw scores, standard scores, developmental scores, percentile ranks, and NCEs (Normal Curve Equivalents) are appropriate for reporting and comparing standardized test results over time. Some data experts believe districts should use all or multiple forms of the same score. Consult your test publisher's manual for information about the scores offered. Test scores are discussed in depth in Chapter 4.

When possible, make sure that the data are entered in their smallest parts. For example, separate name attributes would be set up for "First Name," "Middle Name," and "Last Name," instead of just one "Name" attribute containing first, middle, and last names. Standardized test scores should be entered for each student at the most detailed level available, such as the test item or objective level, which is a level below subscore level. Do not enter calculated data from other attributes at this time (i.e., data that result from adding, subtracting, multiplying, or dividing attribute values). In other words, enter data in "rawest" form. Use raw scores, standard or scaled scores over identifiers of levels of performance (i.e., meets, exceeds, does not meet, except in the case of rubric scores or performance levels that are raw scores). We can always get to performance levels from these scores, but we cannot ever get scaled scores from performance levels.

Backing Up the Files

To ensure the continued maintenance of the database, the database administrator must choose from a variety of ways to back up the database and must standardize when and how the backing up is to be done. The database solution and database architect will recommend when and how routine back-ups get done.

Summary

Data are the essence of the database. Educators need to clarify what data are needed, how they will be used, and the form they are in. The database consultant will determine the attribute specifications—or the details behind the data constructs – with the help of the educators. This work must be done prior to documenting the data specifications and the data model. Remember, building a quality database solution requires:

- keeping the mission and uses in mind at all times
- inputting appropriate data in their smallest and most standardized form
- establishing quality control and back-up procedures

4

TRANSFORMING THE DATA INTO INFORMATION

*Collecting data about a work process has little meaning
to us until we use this data to predict and draw
conclusions about the future, based on the past
performance of this process. Data is value added
only to the extent that it allows us to predict,
and draw conclusions about the future.*

Neil Paulsen
Intel Corporation

We can hand over the database to the database architect to complete
the design and to oversee the importing of data. The most important
job in this quest for schoolwide improvement remains—transforming
the data into useful information that can help school personnel
understand what they need to do to continuously improve.

This chapter focuses on the data analyses desired to answer specific
school improvement questions and the reports that we want the
database to produce. The desired analyses must be clear before the
reports can be generated from the database. In fact, it would assist
the database architects considerably if the desired analyses and reports
are clear before the database design phase begins.

Transforming the Data into Information through Data Analysis

Computers and databases can store data, but only humans can translate those data into real information (see Figure 4.1).

Information is power because it gives us the best alternative to the crystal ball for making predictions that can ultimately prevent future failure and ensure future successes. We will use the database to create analyses that help us understand our current situation, and look for relationships and patterns within the data to inform future decisions. Ironically, and happily, the most useful analyses do not take extensive statistical knowledge. Our goal is not to look for the proverbial "significant differences." Instead, we want to discover and uncover information that will help us understand the data, and the impact of our efforts on our students, determine appropriate interventions and their timing, and to know how to improve everything we do. In other words, information is required to:

- understand where the school/district is right now with respect to student achievement (*overview*)
- *examine* who is and who is not meeting the school/district standards
- *predict* the causes of failures and successes
- and learn what needs to change instructionally to *prevent* future failure and to ensure future successes

General analyses for these four descriptive categories of *overview, examine, predict*, and *prevent* can be developed around logical questions such as the following, which are also shown in Figure 4.2, and described below:

- How well are we doing?
- Are all students succeeding? If not, which ones are not?
- Can we identify students who are at risk of failing so we can intervene?
- What do we need to do differently, early on, to make sure *every* student succeeds in every area?

Figure 4.1

Transforming Data into Information

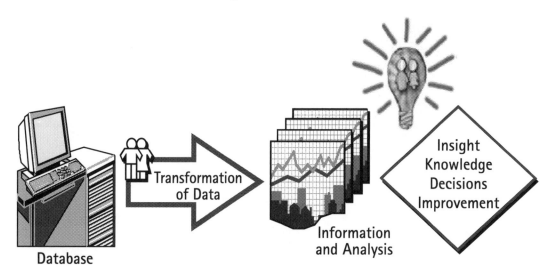

Figure 4.2

General Data Analysis Categories

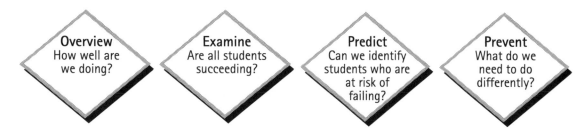

Overview — How Well Are We Doing?

Data needed to understand how well a school is doing with respect to student achievement would come from the student learning category shown in Figure 3.1, Chapter 3—for the current year, and over time. The figures that follow are examples of how the analyses could be graphed to get an overview of how well a school is performing. Figure 4.3 shows student achievement results by subtests by grade level for the entire school for one year only. Figure 4.4 shows student word analysis achievement results by grade level over time.

Figure 4.3

Word Analysis, Concept Development, and Vocabulary Normal Curve Equivalent Scores by Grade, Year One

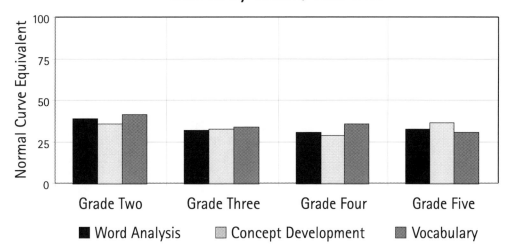

Figure 4.4

Word Analysis Results by Grade for Year One through Year Four

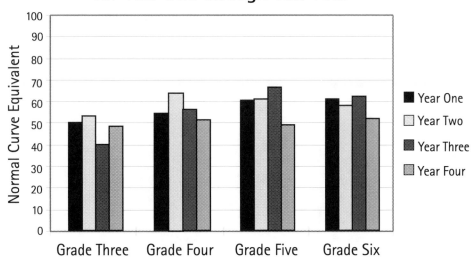

Other general analyses that could be generated from the database to get an overview of results would be graphs of student score distributions for the subtests and total. Figure 4.5 shows the scoring distribution, shown in stanines, for Challenge Elementary School's Fourth Grade Reading Subtest.

Figure 4.5

Scoring Distribution for Challenge Elementary School Grade Four Reading Subtest

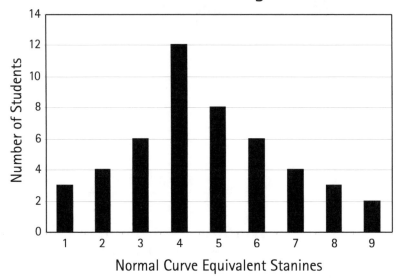

Examine — Are All Students Succeeding?
If Not, Which Ones Are Not?

Digging deeper into the data one can examine two-way and three-way interactions, especially student achievement by demographics, student achievement by school processes, and student achievement by demographics by school processes. These analyses will help us understand if there are particular groups of students having difficulty succeeding in specific subject areas, and/or with specific instructional strategies or programs. Figure 4.6 illustrates a graph of student achievement results by school processes (grade level) over time, following cohorts or groups of students. The graph shows groups of students progressing through the school, from grade to grade. This is an effective approach for following the same students over time, and for seeing the differences in scores between the students who have been there the entire time and those who have moved in and out. From this figure, one can see if all cohorts of students are progressing as expected.

Figure 4.6

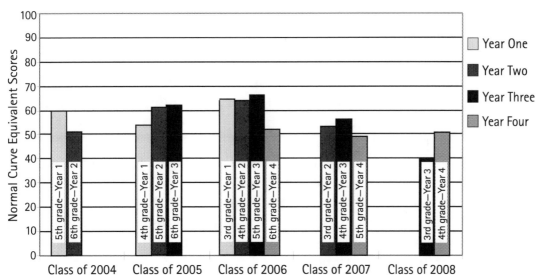

Normal Curve Equivalent Math Scores by Class, Over Time

Figure 4.7 shows the same data as in Figure 4.3 disaggregated by gender. This chart will allow the school to examine performance differences related to gender.

Figure 4.7

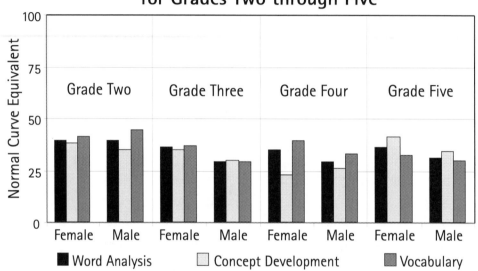

Predict — Can We Identify Students Who Are at Risk of Failing So We Can Intervene?

Data relating to prediction questions would require historical student achievement data intersected with demographics and school processes, in order to locate trends and patterns. Figure 4.8 shows a very special graph created for a classroom. In the chart are individual third grade student scores identified by ethnicity for a reading subtest, along with their second grade, first grade, and pre-first grade scores. From the chart, one can see patterns of learning over time for current third grade students. If done each year, patterns and trends will assist teachers in predicting performance and in adjusting instruction to meet their students' needs.

Figure 4.8

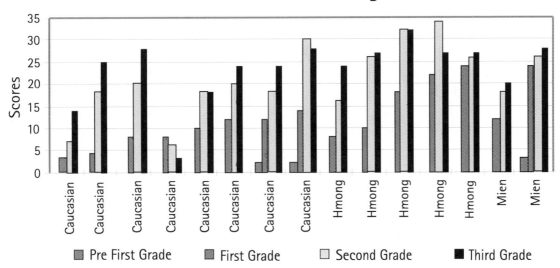

Individual Third Grade Students, Historical Results on Reading Subtest A

Prevent — What Do We Need to do Differently to Make Sure Every Student Succeeds in Every Area?

Our all-time goal of continuous improvement is to understand what needs to be done differently to prevent future failures and to encourage future successes. Data used for prevention would include all prediction data plus perceptions data. Patterns of past performance help teachers predict potential failures. Perceptions data, which might mean a simple interview with students, will help teachers know what to do differently to prevent the failures and ensure successes.

Schools will want to eyeball their data for relationships, patterns, and trends. There is no program that will think through the data for you. Data can be transformed into information only by using the human brain to recognize patterns and trends.

Analysis Related to Multiple Measures

Many schools that qualify for specific federal and/or state funding are required to report student achievement progress in terms of at least three proficiency or achievement levels, over time, and disaggregated by demographics such as gender, ethnicity, and socioeconomic status. These proficiency levels are often referred to as multiple measures of student achievement, or triangulation. The main purpose of using multiple measures is to accurately assess student performance related to standards and then to use the data to improve instruction.

The multiple measures assessments provide students fair, multiple, and varied opportunities to demonstrate what they know and can do. Using multiple measures compensates for the imperfections in every assessment tool.

Examples of multiple measures include:
- Student grades
- Running records
- Norm-referenced tests
- Criterion-referenced tests
- Writing samples
- Oral language samples

When using multiple measures, schools and/or school districts must determine cut scores for each measure, gather the results, and determine if each student is proficient with respect to the standard. An example follows:

> Our Little Elementary School decided to use reading grades, a reading assessment rubric, and normal curve equivalent (NCE) scores from their norm referenced reading assessment as the three multiple measures. They determined to be considered proficient with respect to grades, students must receive a C or higher; with respect to the norm-referenced test, they would have to score at or above 50 NCE; and to be proficient with respect to the reading assessment, they would have to score a four

or higher on the six-point rubric. There were some shades of gray involved as well. They did not want to declare a student proficient if they scored a D or F, or 1 or 2 on the rubric, or 1-29 on the norm-referenced test, even if they exceeded the proficiency levels on the other measures. They designed a chart to help determine quickly and easily if a student is proficient or not.

Table 4.1

Little Elementary School Multiple Measures Chart

Norm-Referenced Test — Normal Curve Equivalent

Grades	Reading Scores	1–29	30–39	40–49	50–59	60+
A	6		Meets Grade-level Standard			
	5		Meets Grade-level Standard			
	4		Meets Grade-level Standard			
	3				Meets Grade-level Standard	
	2					
	1					
Grades	Reading Scores	1–29	30–39	40–49	50–59	60+
B	6		Meets Grade-level Standard			
	5		Meets Grade-level Standard			
	4		Meets Grade-level Standard			
	3				Meets Grade-level Standard	
	2					
	1					

Table 4.1 (Continued)

Little Elementary School Multiple Measures Chart

Norm-Referenced Test — Normal Curve Equivalent

Grades	Reading Scores	1–29	30–39	40–49	50–59	60+
C	6		Meets Grade-level Standard			
	5			Meets Grade-level Standard		
	4				Meets Grade-level Standard	
	3					Meets Grade-
	2					
	1					
Grades	Reading Scores	1–29	30–39	40–49	50–59	60+
D/F	6					
	5					
	4					
	3					
	2					
	1					

Exploratory Analyses

The analyses thus far can be classified as exploratory analyses. The goal of these analyses is generally to explore relationships or to find trends or patterns in numbers representing student achievement scores. Some exploratory analyses are better than others for describing and organizing data. Certainly if one adds the "to what end" or the standard to the analysis, the analyses become more meaningful. Exploratory analyses assist us in finding underlying factors that explain the variation in attributes.

Analyses Related to Standards

One way we can make the general analyses just described more powerful would be to link them to curriculum standards. For example—suppose that teachers want to know more about implementation of a third grade reading standard. Ultimately, they want to be able to answer the following questions:

- What processes are leading students toward meeting the standard by the end of grade three?
- Who and why are some students not meeting the standard by the end of grade three?
- How do student demographics impact these results?
- How does the way students are taught impact the results?
- What do we need to do differently to make sure all students meet the standard by the end of grade three?

School personnel might begin their analysis of the standard with a database of all students at the elementary school. From that database, teachers could look at how the third grade students scored overall. They might then separate the students into two clusters: those who met or exceeded the standard, and those who did not meet the standard. Figure 4.9 illustrates the example for the students who do not meet the third grade reading standard. As one works through the flowchart and digs deeper into the data, one can see how demographics, school processes, and perceptions get included in the conversation to improve the results. A similar figure could be made for the students who meet the standard.

Figure 4.9

A Reading Standard: Grade Three

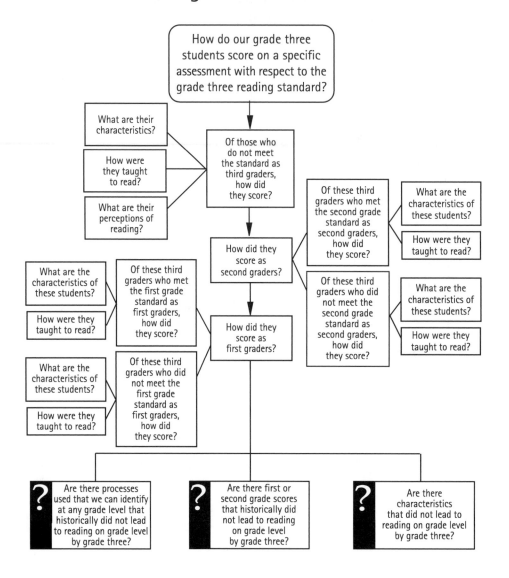

To find out who these students are and how their learning experiences add up to current results, one of the first things educators would want to know is the demographics of the students falling into this category as defined by gender, ethnicity, mobility, home language, socioeconomic status, etc. To learn more about how previous scores relate to third grade scores, each student's second grade scores, as well as first grade scores, could be reviewed. This breakdown could reveal more about the standard, i.e., must students meet the first grade standard at a certain level in order to meet the third grade standard? Must students meet the second grade standard at a certain level in order to meet the third grade standard? In fact, from these breakdowns, one can see whether there are students who met the standard one year and not the next two years, or whether there are students who met the standard for two years and not one year—and determine which year might be the most important for reaching the third-grade standard. Then, by looking at the characteristics of the students by previous scores, one could see if standards attainment is related to language fluency, to one particular element of demographics, or perhaps to the way students are taught. We really cannot know until we dig deeper.

By clustering students in different ways and thinking about how they were taught to read at each grade level (school processes), teachers could become clearer about the results they are getting. Clarifying how results are achieved will also clarify how processes need to be altered to get results that would ensure the success of all students and prevent student failures.

In fact, our ultimate goal in digging deeper is to "predict" and "prevent" student failures. In other words, historical student achievement data can be used to identify factors that can help teachers know when to intervene to prevent potential failure later on. For example, teachers would want to know the answer to the following question: For any subtest or test, are there first or second grade scores that never lead to reading on grade level by grade three?

We might find that any first grader scoring a 12 NCE (Normal Curve Equivalent) on a particular subtest historically never read on grade level by grade three. This would be extremely important information to have. In the following years, if a first grade student scores at 12 or below, teachers would want to intervene to do whatever is necessary to ensure that student's success.

How Can Databases Help with Standards Implementation in the Classroom?

Classroom teachers would benefit from having a database that would allow them to track student progress toward standards attainment throughout the year. Such a database would be supported by the teachers' attention to the processes used to help students achieve the standard. The teachers' ability to recognize processes that need to change would be supported by the information received from the data.

Figure 4.10 is an illustration of questions that can be answered through the use of a classroom database supporting standards implementation. At the beginning of the year, the teacher would identify the standard for the end of the year, including what it would look like when students meet the standard. Additionally, the teacher would start the year with historical assessment information on each student in her classroom. At multiple times during the year, student progress related to the standard would be assessed. At each assessment, the teacher would be able to see who is not making progress toward meeting the standard, to understand if the students not meeting the standard are having difficulty with similar or different concepts, and to intervene with different methods of instruction for those students. The data can also recommend different methods of instruction by looking at what has worked with other students of similar needs and issues.

Figure 4.10

A Third-Grade Reading Standard:
Use Knowledge of Complex Word Families
to Decode Unfamiliar Words

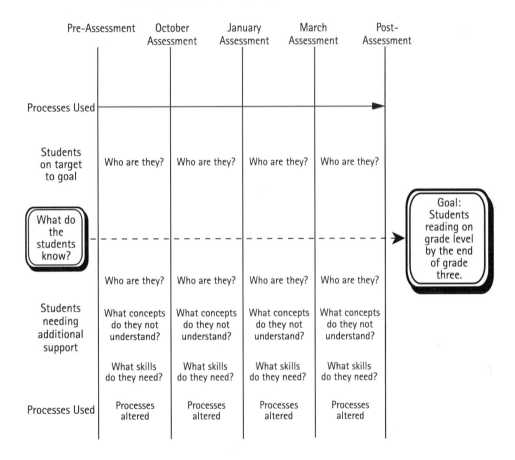

A Note About Processes

It is unfortunate that teachers and administrators do not regularly map their school or classroom processes, or think about processes in relationship to data analyses or the results they are getting. It has been clearly demonstrated that when schools do map their school processes, they can see what needs to change immediately.

Understanding processes (e.g., instruction and assessment strategies, programs) is important because if we want different results, we must change the processes that bring about those results. We cannot continue to do the same things over and over and expect different results.

With respect to reading processes, we often find that schools will assess their students informally (or formally) and then place the bottom 20 percent in individualized instruction (no matter the grade level— elementary, middle, or high school). (See Figure 4.11.) When teachers review their processes in comparison with the results they are getting, they get their "ah-hahs" about what needs to change. Starting with the standard and data, teachers can see that the number of students not meeting the standard might not be 20 percent, it might be more, or less. The process identified in Figure 4.11 would then be incongruent with the needs of the students.

Figure 4.11

Typical Process Flowchart

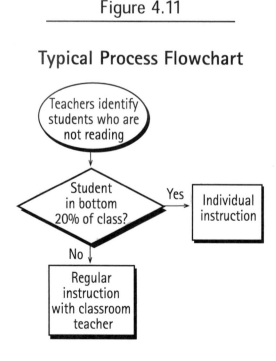

While the beginning flow of Figure 4.12 does not look that much different from Figure 4.11, starting with the standard and data would enable teachers to know exactly how many students need additional work. Instead of thinking in terms of a specific percentage of students to place in individualized instruction, perhaps a new approach to teaching reading must be considered for the classroom and the school.

Figure 4.12

Process Flowchart with Standard

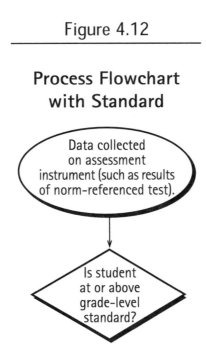

With the use of a database and data analysis, teachers and administrators can understand the congruence of their processes to the needs of the students. With the use of a database and data analysis, teachers and administrators would easily see who is not meeting the standard and what concepts or skills are not being achieved.

Using the "Right" Score

Exploratory analyses can be very powerful and can be created simply. Unfortunately, these analyses are easier to create incorrectly than they are to create correctly. The difference usually stems around using the appropriate scores in the correct manner. Figure 4.13 is a normal curve which is the basis upon which many test scores are developed. The theory of the normal curve is that if a test is given to a group of students, one can expect that few will score very high and few will score very low, with most scoring in the middle, or around the average. At the bottom of Figure 4.13 are the scores that typically are used to describe performance related to the normal curve. The figure shows how the scores relate to each other and to the normal curve. Table 4.2 summarizes typical scores used with norm-referenced standardized achievement tests, the most effective uses of each of the score types and cautions in their uses.

Figure 4.13

The Normal Curve and Scores

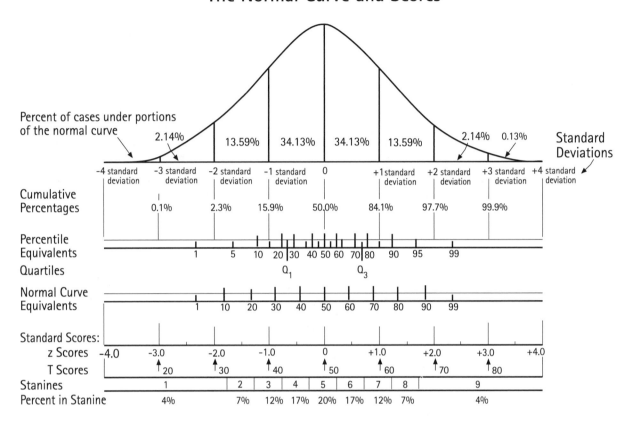

Adapted from Test Service Bulletin No. 48. Copyright © 1955 by The Psychological Corporation.

Table 4.2

Norm-Referenced Test Scores
and Their Most Effective Uses

Score	What It Is	Most Effective Uses	Cautions
Grade-Level Equivalents	The grade and month of the school year for which a given score is the actual or estimated average. Based on a 10-month school year, scores would be noted as 3.1 for grade three, first month, or 5.10 for grade five, tenth month.	Grade-level equivalents are most effectively used as a snapshot in time. Scores are comparable across subtests.	These scores should not be taken literally. If a grade three student scores a 5.8 on a subtest, that does not mean that she/he should be doing grade five, 8th month work. It only means that the student obtained the same score that one would expect average grade five students in their 8th month to score if they were to take the grade three test.
Latent-Trait Scale	A scaled score obtained through one of several mathematical approaches collectively known as Latent-trait procedures or Item Response Theory. The particular numerical values used in the scale are arbitrary, but higher scores indicate more knowledgeable test-takers or more difficult items.	Latent-trait scales have equal intervals allowing for averaging and comparisons over time.	These are scores set up by testing professionals. Lay people typically have difficulty understanding their meaning.
NCE (National or Local)	Normal Curve Equivalent scores are normalized standard scores with a mean of 50 and a standard deviation of 21.06 and a range of 1 to 99.	NCEs have equal intervals so they can be used to study gains over time. The scores have the same meaning across subtests. They can be averaged.	This score, just like all scores related to norm-referenced tests cannot be taken literally. There are no scores that can tell you exactly what students know. These scores are calculated with respect to a group of students, therefore, making them relative to the norm group.

Table 4.2 (Continued)

Norm-Referenced Test Scores and Their Most Effective Uses

Score	What It Is	Most Effective Uses	Cautions
Percentile Rank (PR) or Percentile Equivalent (National or Local)	Percentage of students in a norm group (e.g., national or local) whose scores fall below a given score. Range is from 1 to 99. Fiftieth percentile ranking would mean that 50 percent of the scores in the norming group fall below a specific score. National indicates that the norming group included test takers from across the nation. Local norms are usually test-takers from a state norming group.	Schools can see the relative standing with the norm group of the same grade of the students who took the test at a comparable time.	One cannot calculate averages using PR because of the unequal intervals. Medians are the appropriate statistic to use. Not a score to use over time to look for gains because of unequal intervals, unless the calculations are made with equal interval scores and then converted to percentile ranks.
Quartiles	There are three quartiles— Q1, Q2, Q3 — that divide a distribution into four equal groups: Q1 = 25th percentile Q2 = 50th percentile Q3 = 75th percentile	Quartiles allow schools to see the distribution of scores for any grade level, for instance. Over time, schools trying to increase student achievement would want to monitor the distribution to ensure that all students are moving up.	With quartiles, one cannot tell if the scores are at the top of a quartile or the bottom. There could be "real" changes taking place within a quartile that would not be evident.
Scaled Scores	A mathematical transformation of a raw score.	The best uses of scaled scores are averages and averages calculated over time allowing for the study of change. These scores are good to use for calculations because of equal intervals. The scores can be applied across subtests on most tests. Scaled scores facilitate conversions to other score types.	Ranges vary depending upon the test. Watch for the maximum value. Lay persons sometimes have difficulty finding meaning for these scores. The normal curve is needed to interpret results with respect to other scores and people.

Table 4.2 (Continued)

Norm–Referenced Test Scores
and Their Most Effective Uses

Score	What It Is	Most Effective Uses	Cautions
Standard Scores	A general term referring to scores that have been "transformed" for reasons of convenience, comparability, ease of interpretation, etc. A z-score is a basic standard score with a mean of zero and a standard deviation of one. A z-score is obtained by the following formula: z = (raw score (x) minus the mean), divided by the standard deviation (sd).	Similar to scaled scores, the best uses of standard scores are averages and averages calculated over time, allowing for the study of change. These scores are good to use for calculations because of equal intervals. The scores can be applied across subtests on most tests. Scaled scores facilitate conversions to other score types.	Ranges vary depending upon the test. Watch for the maximum value. These scores are sometimes hard for the lay person to interpret. The normal curve is needed to interpret results with respect to other scores and people taking the same test.
Stanines	A nine-point normalized standard score scale. It divides the normal curve distribution of scores into 9 equal points: 1 to 9. The mean of a stanine distribution is 5 and the standard deviation is approximately 2.	Stanines, like quartiles, allow schools to see the distribution of scores for any grade level, for instance. Over time, schools trying to increase student achievement would want to monitor the distribution to ensure that all student scores are improving.	Often, the first three stanines are interpreted as "below average", the next three as "average", and the top three as "above average". This can be misleading. As with quartiles, one cannot tell if a score is at the top of a stanine or the bottom. There could be "real" changes taking place within a stanine that would not be evident.

Table 4.2 (Continued)

Norm–Referenced Test Scores and Their Most Effective Uses

Score	What It Is	Most Effective Uses	Cautions
T–Scores	A calculated standard score with a mean of 50 and a standard deviation of 10. T-scores are obtained by the following formula: $T = 10z + 50$	Averages and averages calculated over time. Good to use for calculations because of its equal intervals. Can be applied across subtests on most tests because of the forced mean and standard deviation.	T-scores are rarely used because of the lack of understanding on most test users and test interpreters' parts.
z–Scores	A standard score with a mean of zero and a standard deviation of one. z-scores are obtained through the following formula: z = (raw score (x) minus the mean), divided by the standard deviation (sd)	Can indicate how many standard deviations a score is away from the mean.	z-scores are rarely used by the lay public because of the difficulty in understanding the score.

Norm-referenced tests are relatively reliable measures of student achievement. They are beneficial for understanding performance over time. Besides norm-referenced tests, schools use criterion-referenced tests (norm-referenced tests can also be criterion-referenced), performance assessments, grades, and rubric assessments—to name only the most common—to analyze what their students know. Analyses can be conducted using any of these measures, independently and across measures. Common terms and uses of the resulting scores in student achievement analyses are included in Table 4.3.

Table 4.3

Scores and Terms Related to Student Achievement Results and Their Appropriate Uses

Score	What It Is	Most Effective Uses	Cautions
Gain	Gain scores are the change or difference between two administrations of the same test. Gain scores are calculated by subtracting the previous score from the most recent score.	One calculates gains to understand improvements in learning.	Gain scores should not be calculated using unequal interval scores, such as percentiles. Dependent upon the quality of the assessment instrument; the less reliable, the less meaningful.
Maximum	The highest score or the highest possible score on the test.	Maximum possible scores and highest received scores are important for understanding the relative performance of any group or individual.	Tells either the highest score possible or the highest score received by a test-taker. Need to understand which maximum is being used.
Mean	Average score in a set of scores. Calculate by summing all the scores and dividing by the total number of scores.	The mean gives us an overall average for the group taking a specific test. One can use any equal interval score to get a mean.	Means should not be used with unequal interval scores, such as percentile ranks. Means are also sensitive to extreme observations, if there are any.
Median	The score that splits a distribution in half: 50 percent of the scores lie above and 50 percent of the scores lie below the median. If the number of scores is odd, the median is the middle score. If the number of scores is even, one must add the two middle scores and divide by two to calculate the median.	Medians are the way to get an average for scores with unequal intervals. The median splits all scores into two equal parts.	Medians are relative. Probably want to use with the possible and actual maximum and minimum when interpreting medians.
Mode	The score that occurs most frequently in a scoring distribution.	The mode basically tells which score or scores appear most often.	There may be more than one mode.
Minimum	The lowest score or the lowest possible score on the test.	Minimum possible scores and lowest received scores are important for understanding the relative performance of any group or individual.	Tells either the lowest score possible or the lowest score received by a test-taker. Need to understand which minimum is being used.

Table 4.3 (Continued)

Scores and Terms Related to Student Achievement Results and Their Appropriate Uses

Score	What It Is	Most Effective Uses	Cautions
Percent Correct	This is a calculated score implying the percentage of students meeting and exceeding some number, usually a cut score, or a standard. Percent passing = the number passing the test divided by the number taking the test.	With standards-based accountability, it is beneficial to know the percentage of the population meeting and exceeding the standard and to compare a year's percentage with the previous year(s) to understand progress being made.	This is a very simple statistic and its interpretation should be simple as well. Total numbers (n=) of students included in the percentage must always be noted with the percentage to assist in understanding. Ninety percent passing means something very different for 10 or 100 test-takers.
Percent Proficient	Represents the percentage of students who passed a particular test at a "proficient" level, as defined by the test creators, or the test interpreters.	This calculated score can quickly tell educators how well the students are doing with respect to a specific standard. It can also tell educators how many students need additional work to become proficient.	This is a calculated statistic. If used in one year, one will want to keep the calculations in case the standard for proficiency changes. The calculations will be necessary for making recalculations later.
Range	Range is a measure of the spread between the lowest and the highest scores in a distribution. Calculate by subtracting the lowest score from the highest score.	Ranges tell us the width of the distribution of scores. Educators working on continuous improvement will want to watch the range decrease over time.	This is a nice number to know, especially when the maximum and minimum are also taken into consideration.
Raw Scores	Number of questions answered correctly on a test or subtest. Simply calculated by adding the number of questions answered correctly.	The raw score provides information only about the number of questions answered correctly. To get a perspective on performance, raw scores must be used with the average score for the group and the total number of questions. Alone, it has little meaning.	Raw scores do not provide information related to other students taking the test or to other subtests or scores. One needs to keep perspective by knowing the total number possible. Raw scores should never be used to make comparisons between performance on different tests unless other information about the characteristics of the tests is known.

Table 4.3 (Continued)

Scores and Terms Related to Student Achievement Results and Their Appropriate Uses

Score	What It Is	Most Effective Uses	Cautions
Standard Deviation	Measure of variability in a set of scores. The standard deviation indicates how far away scores are from the mean. The standard deviation is the square root of the variance. Unlike the variance, the standard deviation is stated in the original units of the variable. Approximately 68 percent of the scores in a normal distribution lie between plus one and minus one standard deviation of the mean. The more scores cluster around the mean, the smaller the variance.	Tells us about the variability of scores. Standard deviations indicate how spread out the scores are without looking at the entire distribution. A low standard deviation would indicate that the scores of a group are close together. A high standard deviation would imply that the range of scores is wide.	Often this is a confusing statistic for lay persons to understand.
Triangulation	This is a term used for combining three or more measures to get a more complete picture of student achievement.	If students are to be retained based on standards proficiency, educators must have more than one way of knowing if the students are proficient or not. Some students perform well on standardized measures and not on other measures while others do not do well with standardized measures. Triangulation allows students to display what they know on three different measurements.	It is sometimes very complicated to combine different measures to understand proficiency. When the proficiency standards change, the triangulation calculations will need to be revised. Therefore, all the calculations must be documented so they can be recalculated when necessary.

Confirmatory Analyses

Which analyses will tell us if a gain is significant? Confirmatory, or inferential statistical analyses such as t-tests and analyses of variance are conducted to find "real" or significant differences in data groups. Some educators feel that significant differences are very important. Others feel they do not have a place in schoolwide improvement because we are trying to understand how to improve what we are doing for children, not compare groups or programs to each other. Should two groups of students happen to participate in similar programs, one could study the differences in results with confirmatory analyses. Those opposed to the concept of comparisons would say that we could never compare different groups of children to other groups of children because they are different individuals and we cannot account for all the variables that make up the groups, let alone the individuals. Proponents looking for significant differences might want to confirm student achievement gains as being significant, over time. Opponents would say that confirmatory analyses are not necessary for confirming educational gains—any gains are educationally significant.

Statistical significance is only appropriate within the context of inferential statistics (i.e., forming judgements about population parameters by taking samples—usually random) and hypothesis testing. The lay person must first understand hypothesis testing and Type 1 errors to know what significance really means.

With respect to data warehousing or database solutions, you will want to make sure these are options, if your educational organization is a proponent of confirmatory analyses.

What About Data Mining?

Now that the need for databases is becoming more known in the mainstream in education, many terms are being tossed around, some incorrectly. One of these is *data mining*. Educators talk about mining the data or database for answers. Most of the time, they are really just analyzing the data. Data mining is a much more sophisticated term and process. Data mining refers to techniques for finding patterns and trends in very large data sets, which implies well-designed, well-maintained data warehouses. The concept of data mining is becoming increasingly popular as a business information management tool. Its uses in education are not well known, although there would be many—at the state and/or national levels. As database power increases, the amount of available data grows, and the opportunities to use this tool also increases, we will then see more data mining.

Challenge School District

When the Challenge School District database was complete, the database team first looked at their overall standardized test results. They could see that the district was weak in reading both in the early grades and for boys at the high school level. They could also see that girls performed well in science and math, until entering high school. When the scores were disaggregated by schools, they discovered that these phenomena were true at each school—not just some of the schools. By following cohorts of students over time, the analyses revealed that many students were not meeting the reading standards in the very early grades. After digging deeper into the data, the relationships of the variables associated with the reading issue were obvious. The first and foremost issue was language proficiency and processes used to teach reading.

After the district database team analyzed all they could at the district level, they presented each school's data reports to their respective leadership teams. During that session, aggregated and disaggregated charts from the database were given to them with time to study and organize their thoughts and questions. With the support of a district database team member, each leadership team was assisted in determining queries of the database for additional information. The queries were shared across schools to understand common queries that the district could provide in the future. The database team also offered to help facilitate schoolwide meetings so everyone at the school site could participate with the data to determine the next steps.

Summary

Transforming data into information requires generating analyses from the database to help schools get an *overview* of how well they are doing, *examine* the results of the school processes, *predict* which processes are leading to student successes, and *prevent* student failures through these analyses. These analyses begin with general overviews and dig deeper and deeper into the data until student achievement results and the impact of processes are uncovered.

5

TRANSLATING THE INFORMATION INTO SCHOOLWIDE IMPROVEMENT

Schools, classrooms, and school systems can and do improve, and the factors facilitating improvement are neither so exotic, unusual, or expensive that they are beyond the grasp of...ordinary schools.

Larry Lezotte
Learning for All

Our database needs and uses have been identified to design a database that will provide desired information. We have also analyzed and charted the data. Now the information resulting from the data analyses must be translated into plans for comprehensive schoolwide improvement. Fortunately, these data are the same that are required to judge growth and success of the effort—basically, the four multiple measures of data described in Chapter 3: demographics, student learning, perceptions, and school processes. However, how they are analyzed and used depend upon where the school is in its process of school improvement.

Beginning the School Improvement Process

When beginning the school improvement process, data are needed to understand who the students are, and how they are changing over time, the perceptions of students, parents, teachers, and administrators, and current and future needs from everyone's perspective. In addition, data are needed to understand the results of the current processes in order to identify goals for growth. Data required from the database(s) include:

- demographics
- student, graduate, parent, teacher, and administrator perceptions data
- overall student learning results by grade level, and by demographics, e.g., ethnicity, gender, and home language
- student learning results by perceptions, by demographics
- student learning results by school processes, by demographics
- student learning results by school processes, by demographics, by perceptions

Thinking About the Schoolwide Improvement Process

As the school improvement process continues, the use of data shifts to answering questions such as:

- How do we know what to improve?
- How do we use data to prevent failure and ensure success?
- How do we know when improvement has occurred?
- What are our measurement criteria?
- How do we know we are doing the right thing?
- Who will take the lead in our efforts?

According to W. Edwards Deming, systemic improvement occurs when there are fewer failures and more successes. Many educators agree that the distribution of their student performance could resemble the normal curve, like Figure 5.1. When visualizing the distribution they are trying to form through school improvement, educators visualize a distribution that would have only high performers, similar to Figure 5.2

Figure 5.1

The Normal Distribution

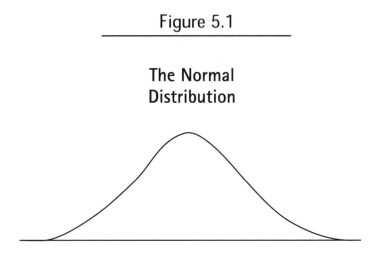

Figure 5.2

Some Educators' Desired Distribution

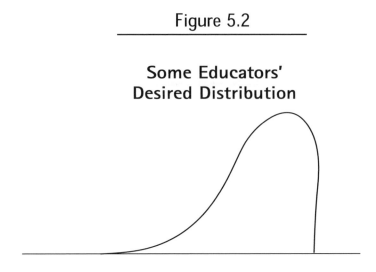

If we are decreasing the failures and increasing the successes, in other words improving all scores, the resulting distribution would not be skewed like Figure 5.2. It would still resemble the normal curve, however, the whole curve would move to the right, as illustrated in Figure 5.3. This would mean that the school improvement process succeeded in improving the performance of students from every point in the distribution—hopefully, every student.

Figure 5.3

Changes in Student Achievement Distribution through Continuous Improvement

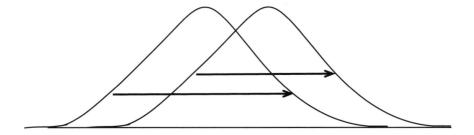

No school can truly improve systemically if all aspects of the system are not taken into account. Changing one part of the system is not systemic change. Implementing parts without regard to the system can be referred to as implementing random acts of improvement as opposed to focused acts of improvement (Figure 5.4).

Figure 5.4

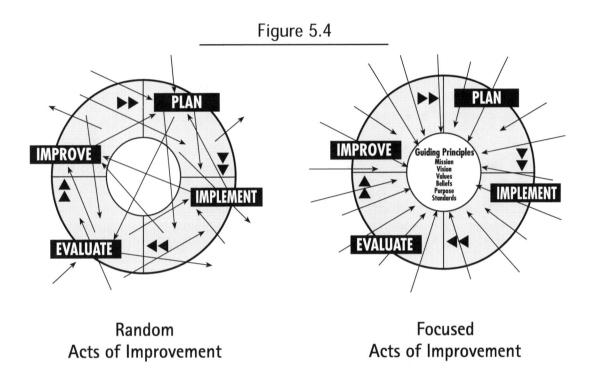

Random
Acts of Improvement

Focused
Acts of Improvement

For example, high school personnel targeting increasing dropout rates would likely decrease the number of dropouts with the implementation of a dropout prevention program. However, it is then conceivable that the school's student achievement scores might consequently decrease because lower performing students would now be retained in school and their scores would be included in the school average. One does not want to improve the dropout rate and then have the school board decry the low achievement scores. Additionally, one must bring the school board, public, and news media along as the strategy is planned, and clarify the predicted results—good and bad.

In the case of this high school, staff would need to improve *all* processes for *all* students—not just target their high dropout rate to get to schoolwide improvement (i.e., target increased student achievement for *all* students in addition to implementing an intervention program).

To systemically improve, school personnel must clarify the guiding principles of the school (i.e., vision, mission, standards) and aim all improvements toward this focus. Gathering data clarifies what to improve, allows staff to measure the effectiveness of what they are currently doing, and informs them of their alignment with the school's guiding principles. At all times, school processes, improvements, and evaluations need to be assessed within the context of these guiding principles.

In an effort to ensure that school processes are in alignment with guiding principles, data need to be gathered about the guiding principles themselves. Perceptions of teachers could answer questions related to a shared vision, a mission, values and beliefs, and leadership. If the data show there is no shared vision, the school community must either revisit the vision, or continue to work on a vision they can share.

Summary

Using data to help schools know how to prevent failure and improve every student's chances for success is exactly where continuously improving schools must focus their energies. These types of analyses rely on quality databases, on credible and reliable measures of student knowledge and abilities, and consistent and high quality indicators and assessment systems. With a database that follows individual student progress over time, staff can begin to understand what each student is experiencing and understand the impact of school processes and the learning environment on student learning results. With this information, teachers can begin to ask questions of the data that will help them determine what they need to do differently to decrease failures and increase successes. By focusing on student learning standards, teachers can query the database to understand the characteristics of students who are failing, and to understand the concepts which they are failing in order to intervene to ensure their successes. Historical data provide powerful indicators which can be used to identify struggling students so their potential failures can be prevented. Data can be used further to clarify where every student is with respect to a learning standard, which then enables staff to know what each student requires for improvement, not just those students who are failing.

6

USING THE DATABASE AT ALL LEVELS — DISTRICT, SCHOOL, CLASSROOM

> *If we set specific goals and honestly and systematically commit ourselves to achieving them, we will almost invariably improve.*
>
> **Mike Schmoker**
> *Results: The Key to Comprehensive School Improvement*

With the database design and analyses clarified, we are right back to where we started—thinking about the users of and the uses for the data. In this chapter we present examples of teachers and districts using data to improve what they are doing for children. These examples are included to encourage teachers and administrators to get started on data analysis and database work wherever they are.

San Jose Unified School District

San Jose Unified School District (SJUSD) with 33,000 students in 43 schools has been addressing the construction of a seamless, comprehensive student achievement database and a user-friendly software interface which allows administrators and staff in all schools to obtain up-to-the minute, disaggregated student data to assist them in targeting their continuous improvement efforts. Data teams of administrators and teachers have been trained to drill down into their site data. They create pivot tables and charts using any possible combination of demographic and student achievement data they think might be important to their program evaluation. Having clear data about specific populations of students has been revelatory and empowering for the schools. Principals say that this is what they have most needed to help them run their schools more effectively. Teachers say that it helps them determine which instructional strategies positively impact student learning. All are understanding data's power to validate their efforts and to determine and address the root causes of student failure.

Laurens County School District 56

Laurens County School District 56 in Clinton, South Carolina, built a data warehouse with the help of a South Carolina database company. The warehouse server holds all of the district data, and with easy querying tools, the superintendent can print out in seconds standard reports that used to take months to create, call up historical information about any school, program, process, or grade level, disaggregate on the fly, and see the system in ways that were not possible before. This data warehouse is allowing all parts of the district to understand the impact of their actions on students and to focus professional development and other dollars on areas of most need.

River Road High School

A few years ago, River Road High School teachers committed themselves and their school to a continuous improvement process with the ultimate goal of increasing student learning. As they reviewed their school level data, provided by their district, they could see what every teacher already knew—River Road students were not doing well in writing. The teachers commiserated one more time about how the ninth graders come to them from middle school as poor writers. One thing was different this time, their new continuous improvement process would not allow them to get by with making excuses and then doing the same thing they have always done. After reviewing the average achievement scores from the middle schools that feed into the high school, the teachers realized those data were not enough information with which to make decisions about necessary changes. They knew if they really wanted to use data to improve, they would need individual student scores, and they needed a measurement tool to use throughout the year to measure progress. Here is what they did:

- The teachers determined where they wanted every freshman to be by the end of the freshman year with respect to writing proficiency.

- Working backward, the teachers calculated where the students needed to be with respect to writing proficiency in March, January, and November in order to meet that year-end goal.

- They then designed a writing assessment that was given to all freshmen as they entered River Road High School.

- They built their instruction based on the skill levels of the students they had in their classrooms and measured again in November.

- One of the teachers built a database for the teachers to enter their assessment results.

- The teachers studied the progress of their students and graphed the interim results against their predictions.

- The teachers altered their instruction to keep the students on target with the writing proficiency goal.

- They measured and discussed best approaches to get all their freshmen proficient in writing.

- By the end of the year they had met their writing proficiency goals.

- The next year, the same process was used with sophomores, juniors, and seniors.
- In the following year, the process began to be used in other subject areas, as the school database was being designed to make this ongoing assessment a part of what they do.
- In that same year, the English teachers began to collaborate with middle school teachers on what grade seven and eight teachers might emphasize to get students "ready" for grade nine.

The teachers loved looking at the results and seeing the impact of their actions on the students. They thought the ongoing measurement and graphing against goals was fun and that the data sparked meaningful and productive discussions. It was the first time in most of these seasoned veterans' careers that the teachers actually talked about teaching whenever they saw each other. It was the first time that the English teachers willingly met after school to talk about teaching. These teachers were convinced that the data made the difference. It was objective, real, and inspiring. It kept them going.

These English teachers fell into a database situation. Their little database helped them follow individual student progress during the year and achieve just about any goal they set. Within two years, the entire school staff figured out they needed an official database to support their ongoing measurements. How could the administration refuse their request? The administration would do whatever was needed to get it set up and make it easy to use. The student achievement increases were wonderful.

Another School District

In another district, one administrator worked with teachers to build ongoing authentic assessment measures related to newly developed standards. She knew the teachers would benefit from immediate analyses and viewing of their class results; in addition, she wanted these analyses to be used with the standardized test results in the district database. If the schools and the district had been networked with computers for every teacher, she might have figured out a way for the teachers to enter their assessments into an online database. She did know, however, how to design questionnaires for optical scanning. Using this knowledge, the administrator designed optical scanner readable forms for teachers to darken in circles related to individual student assessments. The administrator scans the forms into a database and uses templates to get analyses in chart form. She gets the results back to the teachers on the same day they do the assessments.

Student Performance Monitoring System

The Student Performance Monitoring System (SPMS) was developed by two building level administrators in Ohio to help teachers and administrators implement statewide educational standards. The SPMS is a relational database system that warehouses and retrieves student information in a user-friendly, Web-based environment that enables educators to conduct in-depth analyses of student performance. The power and utility of the SPMS is the graphing and reporting of student performance on both state-mandated proficiency testing and locally developed, curriculum-based, benchmark assessments. Reporting screens permit point and click "instant" querying of student information that gives the user multiple views and reports of all student data warehoused in the database system. This kind of accessible data analyses enable educators to analyze student information from multiple measures to identify patterns of learning that otherwise may be overlooked.

Homegrown Database Systems

The majority of school districts in the United States serve fewer than 500 students. A comprehensive data warehouse would neither be affordable nor appropriate for this size. However, a database would still be desirable and useful.

Many small school districts must rely on commercial software that they customize to include their data. Many of the principles discussed in Chapter 2 are relevant. The hardest part of a homegrown system is to query the data quickly. Data managers must think through the data and figure out the analyses and reports that they want.

Making Data Accessible to Teachers

Many times we hear teachers and principals bemoaning the fact that their district has tons of data, but all they get are annual, canned reports that are neither timely nor useful to them. They ask for specific data, and depending upon who is in charge of the district database, they may get it, or they may not. Even if these forward-thinking teachers get their special requested reports, the other schools in the district probably will not get any additional reports because the district data person just physically cannot generate the reports—in the current mode of operation, that is. My staff and I have had numerous discussions with district data administrators. It seems they are convinced that teachers will not look at or use the data they are capable of giving them. Thus, they stay in their current mode of operation.

We know that most district data services offices cannot do everything for all schools—right now. However, we must convince them to change their thinking and remind them about why we are all here—to assist students in their learning. So, if teachers want to use data to improve instruction for students, these offices should be trying their hardest to make it happen. At the same time, we must convince some teachers of the benefits of using data at the individual student level. With those two belief systems in place, we can proceed with making the job possible.

District personnel often think that if they hire someone to supply paper reports, they will avoid security problems. This works until people at the site start using data regularly. Good data almost always leads to a demand for more good data, causing a bottleneck if those who want the data do not have direct access.

One approach to a win-win solution for both would be for the district office to make school level data available to each school and teacher. The schools could then generate their special reports and dig deeper into the data. This sounds easy enough, although it is not easy without a database tool that will allow for point-and-click querying. The tools are now available. They are worth the investment. That is the only way schools and districts will be able to generate the reports that are needed to understand more about improving student achievement.

Summary

Teachers who use data in an ongoing fashion love to watch their students' progress. Teachers want data. Teachers will use it for the benefit of students. Districts must do what they can to get quality data in the hands of school administrators and teachers—with a high-end data warehouse or a "homegrown" database.

7

SUMMARY AND CONCLUSIONS

In the last decade, we as a nation, spent billions of dollars on school improvement, with limited success. Most of the schools that successfully improved their organizations and increased student achievement scores can credit their successes to the use of data. Contrary to some opinions, educators want to use data. They just do not have access to quality data when they need and want it—in a user-friendly manner. A quality data warehouse located at the school district level can provide the district, its administrators, and its teachers with access to the data that will help each level of the organization continuously improve. Actually, any database that will allow teachers to access and manipulate historical student achievement in combination with school process and demographic data is beneficial. What follows is a summary review of the steps and issues in the design of a database or data warehouse.

Building a Database

Although the building of a data warehouse is detail-oriented requiring a lot of up-front work and commitment, the finished product will make all users' lives easier in the end.

Additionally the process itself is valuable because it forces the players to communicate, collaborate, and create a solution that is good for everybody.

Start with a Strong Foundation

The actual data warehouse needs to be designed on paper before any data is touched or processed. Start by determining the *mission* of the database and by *identifying a committee* to design the database.

The *mission* is the focus of the project and along with quantifiable goals and objectives, keeps everyone grounded. The mission should clearly state the purpose of the database. For example: The mission of the Challenge Unified School District's database is to support district and school goals to improve student learning by generating information for analysis in user-friendly formats for continuous improvement.

Identify a committee to design the database, to synthesize the uses, and to anticipate the needs of all potential users. The database design committee needs to include a representative group of users and database engineers, including, but not limited to, a database designer, data archaeologist, and systems programmer:

- Users are those people who will want to access the data from the data warehouse for specific purposes. As committee members, they will give a realistic perspective of the needs of the users. Users include, but are not limited to, teachers, program directors, data entry clerks, administrators, school board members, and the general public.
- Database designers have an understanding of database hardware and software and can mold the database around the needs of the users and requirements of the data.

- Data archaeologists locate, scrub, reconcile, and understand the data. Up to 60 percent of the effort will be spent in this area. These people will make sure that meaningful data get entered into the database or data warehouse, so that meaningful data can be retrieved from the database.
- Systems programmers are a necessity to get and keep data flowing smoothly into the data warehouse. Including them in the design will alleviate problems later.

Decisions the committee must make include the following:

- Refine the mission, if it was begun before all committee members were identified.
- Determine all uses for the database. This will include listing the reports required by the state, program officers, and district. Also included would be the many uses by teachers and administrators. It is critical to identify all potential uses and their data requirements before starting the design, if possible. It will help clarify the data needed to be included and the analyses required.
- Determine the data that exist and the form that they are in.
- Identify additional data that will need to be included in the database.
- Determine who is going to do the work. The database or data warehouse will not stand alone. It will need maintenance and updating. End users will need support and training, and the data will need to be imported or input into the database.
- Identify how quality and security will be maintained.
- Clarify the data analyses which should be closely related to the purpose and mission.
- Document the design. Every decision about the database needs to be documented so anyone can find out why decisions were made and what each element stands for.
- Determine who will have access to the database and how.
- Determine the solutions in which to invest.

Expect to spend some money on the upfront costs. Also expect to spend money on maintenance, updates, and training.

Database Solutions

Those of us in education are used to buying a piece of software, and with little or no training, take off and run with it. With relational databases, we are in a totally different ball game. For one, there will not be one piece of software that will do everything related to a data warehouse that is discussed in this book. Most probably, you will hear discussions about three pieces of software that will be required: a database manager, a graphical user interface, and a graphical report tool.

A database manager defines what the data will look like and automatically gathers all pertinent information from a variety of formats, such as ASCII and ODBC, into an OLAP structure and places them into tables or cubes. (Words are defined in the Glossary of Terms.)

This data manager will transfer the data into a SQL server database without hours spent entering each piece of data. You will want to make sure the data manager provides for visual checks and validation to filter out bad data, and that it cannot delete or damage data in the system.

A Graphical User Interface (GUI) enables drill-down and drill-up multidimensional functionality with easy data manipulation. This piece is most commonly networked with a server. You want a database design that will sort, select, disaggregate and aggregate on the server and not on the user's computer desktop. Analyzing on the server will be fastest, since analyzing on the users' desktop would imply moving the data. This client-server design enables the analysis of large amounts of data quickly. The client sends a request to the server telling the server what questions she/he wants answered. The server processes the request by searching the database and returning only the answer that the client requested. In this way, most of the processing takes place on the server and only a minimum amount of information is transmitted across the network.

One of the most easily overlooked tasks of the data warehouse project is the selection of end user tools. You will want a tool that is intuitive to all end users and one that can graph the results. The goal should be to allow anyone who wants to use data to access the database on their own without requiring a database coordinator to help them or to do it for them. We want the end user to spend her/his time understanding the data analysis results, not learning the tools to get the data into an understandable form. We need to encourage self-sufficiency. Our end desire is to get teachers and administrators using data regularly because the information they can get out of the database will make their jobs easier and allow them to be more efficient with students.

The End User

The typical educational end users could be categorized as Report Viewers, Data Tourists, and Information Surfers. Report Viewers are those who look for answers in the same place on the same report, at the same time. This group is often best served by standard reports. Group members might be our Boards of Education. Data Tourists would need help getting started, but are not afraid to strike off on their own when they've grown comfortable. They can investigate data with point and click querying. Most teachers and administrators would probably fall into this category. Information Surfers will want fast answers to questions no matter where they are. Standard reporting solutions rarely satisfy these folk. These are most probably the staff of our district and regional research and evaluation offices.

Maintaining and Administering the Data Warehouse

Certainly the administration of the data warehouse grows in complexity as the size of the database and the number of users increase. Data warehouses are never complete. They grow systematically and require continuous effort to keep them running smoothly and to respond to the requirements of the end users. Avoid thinking there is a one-size-fits-all solution. Incorporate system flexibility in your database solution. For one, no one knows what we forgot to take into consideration. Two, no one knows what will be needed in five or ten years.

Please remember that the reason we are doing this work to select a database solution is that we want extraordinary results for our students. Don't forget to document the results. Publish the best uses and best results. Encourage the use and the results.

Summary

Real school improvement with significant student achievement increases can be realized through the use of data. School personnel believe and understand this. The problem is that teachers and administrators typically do not have the data available in accessible forms. Everyone in a school district would benefit from having a data warehouse that would allow district, school, and classroom educators to access and use the data. Teachers would love to have historical or even last year's student achievement data on this year's students. Imagine how much more focused they could be in making sure every student succeeds in reaching standards.

Without data, districts, schools, and classroom teachers are merely guessing at the changes that are needed in order to get different results. Without a database, these entities might as well not have any data because it would be impossible to correctly look at trends, or to dig deep into the data to understand instructional impacts on special populations. With a database, districts can understand the impact of their administrative decisions on all the district's schools and students. With a database, schools can understand what they can do differently to get different results.

APPENDIX:
DATABASE NEEDS
ANALYSIS TOOL

The Database Needs Analysis Form (see Figure A-1 on the following pages) is an assessment tool for determining database needs.

The intent of this tool is to help school and school district personnel think through all that must be taken into account as they search for database solutions. While the form may imply a linear format, considering database needs is dynamic.

The form starts out by asking who needs to be on the committee to design the database. This is not the only time this question should be asked. It will need to be revisited as more and more information about purposes and uses are gathered.

Refer to Chapter 2 for more details about this form and to read an example of using the form.

Figure A-1

DATABASE NEEDS ANALYSIS FORM

1 Determine the mission, goals, and objectives of the database.

2 Identify who should be on the committee to assist with the design of the database.

3 Clarify the role of the committee, including timelines.

4 Determine purposes, uses, users, and data requirements.

Figure A-1 (Continued)

DATABASE NEEDS ANALYSIS FORM

(5) Identify the database software that is being used in the district and school offices.

(6) Describe the current networking system.

(7) Describe what the software should do that is not now being done by current practices.

(8) Describe the data that are currently available.

(9) Determine how much has been budgeted for this work.

Figure A-1 (Continued)

DATABASE NEEDS ANALYSIS FORM

(10) Describe the data you want to include in the database.

(11) Select the database design team.

(12) Identify who will input the data.

(13) Identify who will produce the standard reports.

Figure A-1 (Continued)

DATABASE NEEDS ANALYSIS FORM

14 Identify who will maintain the database.

15 Determine the levels of access, who will have access at each level, and how access will be obtained.

GLOSSARY OF TERMS

This glossary provides brief definitions of data analysis, data warehousing, and database terms.

Aggregate
Combining the results of all groups that make up the sample or population.

ASCII
An acronym for American Standard Code for Information Interchange. ASCII is an industry-standard, text-only file format.

Attribute
Otherwise known as a field, an attribute is a characteristic of the entity, such as name, ethnicity, or gender.

Attribute Specifications
Specifications that control the kind of information that can be entered into the attribute, such as data type (e.g., number, text, or date) or properties (e.g., field size, format, and validation rule).

Authentic Assessments
Refers to a variety of ways to evaluate a student's demonstration of knowledge and skills, but does not include traditional testing. Authentic assessments may include performances, projects, exhibitions, and portfolios.

Cohort
Refers to a group of individuals sharing a particular statistical or demographic characteristic, such as the year they were in a specific school grade level. Following cohorts over time helps us understand the effects particular circumstances may have on results. Matched cohort studies follow the same individuals over time and unmatched cohort studies follow the same group over time.

Column
Represents one attribute (field) of the entity.

Criterion-referenced Tests

Tests that judge how well a test taker does on an explicit objective relative to a pre-determined performance level. There is no comparison to any other test takers.

Cube

Cube is the term used to describe a database for multidimensional analysis. Each cube contains a set of measures (quantitative data) and dimensions (descriptive data such as grade). Queries are sent to the cube to be answered.

Cube Browser

User interface for browsing data that is stored in an OLAP cube. This software is meant as an exploratory tool.

Data Archaeologist

A person whose job it is to locate and "cleanse" historical data before the data are entered into the database. Data archaeologists verify data accuracy and consistency and make the data compatible and relatable.

Data Cleansing

The process of ensuring that all values in a dataset are consistent and correctly recorded.

Data Cubes

Multidimensional representations of relational data, usually created using a star or snowflake schema. Each cube can be its own database (also see cube, above).

Data Mart

A subset of a data warehouse that focuses on one or more specific subject areas. The data usually are extracted from the data warehouse and further denormalized and indexed to support intense usage by targeted customers.

Data Mining

Techniques for finding patterns and trends in large data sets. The process of automatically extracting valid, useful, previously unknown, and ultimately comprehensible information from large databases.

Data Model

The road map to the data in a database. This includes the source of tables and columns, the meanings of the keys, and the relationships between the tables.

Data Visualization

Techniques for turning data into information by using the high capacity of the human brain to recognize visually, patterns and trends.

Data Warehouse

A database built to support information access. Typically a data warehouse is fed from one or more transaction databases. The data need to be cleansed and restructured to support queries, summaries, and analyses.

Database

A storage mechanism for data that eliminates redundancy and conflict among multiple data files. Data is entered once and is then available to all programs that need it.

Database Management System (DBMS)

A series of programs that manage large sets of data. The DBMS may control the organization, storage, and retrieval of data in a database, in addition to controlling the security and integrity. The three most common types of a DBMS are hierarchical, network, and relational.

Database Designer or Database Architect or Database Engineer

Person who creates the ERDs for a relational database system. The database designer should have coursework and experience in computer science, statistics, and education.

Deciles

The values of a variable that divide the frequency distribution into ten equal frequency groups. The ninth decile is the value below which 90 percent of the norming group lie.

Demographics

Statistical characteristics of a population, such as average age, number of students in a school, percentages of ethnicities, etc. Disaggregation with demographic data allows us to isolate variations among different subgroups.

Denormalization

Consists of the inclusion of derived data, the merging of tables, and the creation of arrays of data. One would denormalize by sacrificing some normalization to achieve speed increases.

Dimension

A dimension is a structural attribute of a cube that is a list of members, all of which are of a similar type in the user's perception of the data. A dimension acts as an index for identifying values within a multi-dimensional array. Dimensions offer a very concise, intuitive way of organizing and selecting data for retrieval, exploration, and analysis.

Disaggregate

Separating the results of different groups that make up the sample or population.

Drill-down

An OLAP (online analytical processing) feature educators will want to use the most. It essentially allows for the disaggregation of data in a quick, easy-to-use manner. As desired, one can dig deeper and deeper into the data and into increasing levels of detail.

Drill-up

An OLAP feature that does the opposite of the drill-down. Going from the smallest level of detail to higher and higher levels.

ECTL

The extract, cleanse, transform, and load process for getting data into the database.

Entity Relation Diagram (ERD)

Represent the arrangement and relationship of data entities for the logical data structure. ERDs are created to reduce redundant data. Star Schema and Snowflake Schema are ERDs.

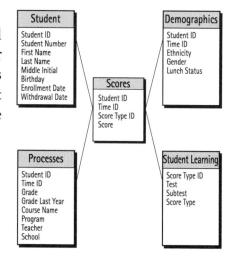

Frequency Distribution

A frequency distribution describes how often observations fall within designated categories. It can be expressed in either numbers or percent.

Gain Score

Gain scores are the change of difference between two administrations of the same test. Gain scores are calculated by subtracting the previous score from the most recent score.

Grade-level Equivalent

The grade and month of the school year for which a given score is the actual or estimated average. Based on a 10-month school year, scores would be noted as 3.1 for grade three, first month, or 5.10 for grade five, tenth month.

Graphical User Interface

The use of pictures (e.g., icons, buttons, dialog boxes, etc.) to manipulate the input and output of programs. The user selects objects with a pointer, usually controlled with a mouse.

Import Manager

A piece of software that allows the user to import data into a database from other sources.

Join

A special type of query that combines data from more than one table. This is a key feature of relational databases. An inner join selects rows from two tables such that the value in one column of the first table also appears in a certain column of the second table. For an outer join, the results also includes all rows from the first operand ("left outer join", "*="), or the second operand ("right outer join", "=*"), or both ("full outer join", "*=*")."

Latent Trait

A scaled score obtained through one of several mathematical approaches collectively known as Latent-trait procedures or Item Response Theory. The particular numerical values used in the scale are arbitrary, but higher scores indicate more knowledgeable test takers or more difficult items.

Maximum

The highest actual score or the highest possible score on the test.

Mean

Average score in a set of scores. Calculate by summing all the scores and dividing by the total number of scores.

Median

The score that splits a distribution in half: 50 percent of the scores lie above and 50 percent of the scores lie below the median. If the number of scores is odd, the median is the middle score. If the number of scores is even, one must add the two middle scores and divide by two to calculate the median.

Meta-data

Basically the descriptive information about the data in the database—data about data. Metadata describe the structure and relationships of data pieces. This includes such items as the names of the source fields that the data come from, the calculations to transform the data before loading it into the target database, the names of the columns that the data are going into in the target database, and meaningful end-user oriented descriptions of the target database tables and columns.

Minimum

The lowest score or the lowest possible score on the test.

Mode

The score that occurs most frequently in a scoring distribution.

Normal Curve Equivalent (NCE)

Equivalent scores are standard scores with a mean of 50 and a standard deviation of 21.06 and a range of 1 to 99.

Normal Distribution

Also known as a normal curve, it is a bell-shaped distribution of scores where most of the scores group in the middle.

Normalization

The process of decomposing large tables (files) into smaller tables in order to eliminate redundant data and duplicate data, and to avoid problems with inserting, updating, and deleting data. Normalization is a way of organizing the data to prevent data duplication and to preserve strict relationship semantics.

Normalized Standard Score

A transformation procedure used to make scores from different tests more directly comparable. Not only is the mean and standard deviation of the raw score distribution changed, as with a linear standard score transformation, but the shape of the distribution is converted to a normal curve. The transformation to a normalized z-score involves two steps: 1) compute the exact percentile rank of the raw score; and 2) determine the corresponding z-score for that exact percentile rank from a table of areas under the normal curve.

Norm-referenced Tests

Tests in which the scores are compared to a norm group, a representative sample of a specified population.

Norms

Representative standards or values for a given group against which individual scores can be compared.

ODBC

Open database connectivity is a Microsoft standard, now adopted by most database programs, that allows a database, spreadsheet and other programs to link to ODBC compliant databases. It then allows for the importing/exporting of data.

OLAP

Online analytical processing, refers to tools developed to store data sets retrieved from databases that allow users to see the data in multi-dimensional formats. OLAP tools are not databases and, unlike data mining tools, OLAP tools do not learn or create new knowledge.

OLTP

Online transaction processing, the technology that allows access to a small number of tables during a given transaction.

Percentile Rank (PR)

Percentage of students in a norm group (e.g., national or local) whose scores fall below a given score. Range is from 1 to 99. A 50th percentile ranking would mean that 50 percent of the scores in the norming group fall below a specific score.

Percent Correct

A calculated score implying the percentage of students meeting and exceeding some number, usually a cut score, or a standard. Percent passing = the number passing the test divided by the number taking the test.

Percent Proficient

Represents the percentage of students who passed a particular test at a "proficient" level, as defined by the test creators, or the test interpreters.

Perceptions Data

Information that reflects opinions and views of questionnaire responses.

Pivot Table

A statistical software program output table, which summarizes data, that can be pivoted interactively. Some pivoting options include rearranging rows and columns, creating multidimensional layers, and showing and hiding cells.

Primary Key

An attribute(s) that uniquely identifies one record from another.

Processes

Measures that describe what is being done to get results, such as programs, strategies, and practices.

Quartiles

There are 3 quartiles—Q1, Q2, Q3—that divide a distribution into 4 equal groups (Q1=25th percentile; Q2=50th percentile; Q3=75th percentile).

Query

A request one makes to a database that is returned to the desktop. Understanding and knowing how to set up queries or to ask questions of the database is very important to the information discovery process.

Raw Scores

A person's observed score on a test or subtest. Number of questions answered correctly on a test or subtest. Simply calculated by adding the number of questions answered correctly.

Range

Range is a measure of the spread between the lowest and the highest scores in a distribution. Calculate by subtracting the lowest score from the highest score.

Relational Database

A type of database that allows the definition of data structures, storage, and retrieval operations and integrity constraints (requirements that must be satisfied for the database to maintain integrity). The data and relations between them are stored in table form. Relational databases are powerful because they require few assumptions about how data are related and how they will be extracted from the database.

Row

Represents one occurrence of an entity (record.) A row is the horizontal line in a table.

Rubric

A scoring tool that rates performance according to clearly stated levels of criteria. The scales can be numeric or descriptive. For instance, school process rubrics are used to give schools an idea of where they started, where they want to be with respect to implementation, and where they are right now.

Scaled Scores

A mathematical transformation of a raw score.

Snowflake Schema

A database architecture for building cubes. The snowflake schema divides the dimension tables into multiple tables, by reintroducing a level of normalization.

Structured Query Language (SQL)

Structured Query Language is the standard database language used by database programs. In most database programs, actions you take to add and retrieve data are converted behind the scenes to SQL commands to communicate your requests between and among database tables.

Standard Deviation

Measure of variability in a set of scores. The standard deviation is the square root of the variance. Unlike the variance, the standard deviation is stated in the original units of the variable. Approximately 68 percent of the scores in a normal distribution lie between plus one and minus one standard deviation. The more scores cluster around the mean, the smaller the variance.

Standard Scores

A group of scores having a desired mean and standard deviation. A z-score is a basic standard score. Other standard scores are computed by first converting a raw score to a z-score (sometimes normalized), multiplying the transformation by the desired standard deviation, and then adding the desired mean to the product. The raw scores are transformed this way for reasons of convenience, comparability, and ease of interpretation.

Standardized Tests

Tests that are uniform in content, administration, and scoring. They can be used for comparing results across classrooms, schools, school districts, and states.

Standard

Something that is considered as a basis of comparison or a guideline that is used as a basis for judgement.

Stanines

A nine-point normalized standard score scale. It divides the normal curve distribution of scores into nine equal points: 1 to 9. The mean of a stanine distribution is 5 and the standard deviation is approximately 2.

Star Schema

A popular database architecture for building cubes. A star schema model consists of fact tables surrounded by and related to dimension tables. Fact tables contain the information that you report and analyze.

Student Achievement Data

Information that reflects a level of knowledge, skill, or accomplishment, usually in something that has been explicitly taught.

Systems Programmer

A non-specific job title that encompasses a variety of specialist roles. Typically, experience in specific operating systems, networking, electronic mail, operating and network security, and hardware devices are required.

T-Score

A calculated standard score with a mean of 50 and a standard deviation of 10. T-scores are obtained by the following formula: $T=10z+50$. T-scores are sometimes normalized.

Table

A data structure for relational databases, comprised of rows and columns, like a spreadsheet.

Triangulation

Term used for combining three or more measures to get a more complete picture of student achievement.

Variance

A measure of the dispersion, or variability, of scores about their mean. The population variance is calculated by taking the average of the squared deviations from the mean—a deviation being defined as an individual score minus the mean.

z-Score

A standard score with a mean of zero and a standard deviation of one. A z-score is obtained by the following formula: z = raw score (x) minus the mean, divided by the standard deviation (sd). A z-score is sometimes normalized.

REFERENCES AND RESOURCES

Adriaans, P. & Zantinge, D. (1996). *Data Mining*. White Plains, NY: Addison-Wesley Longman.

Barker, J. (1992). *Paradigms: The Business of Discovering the Future*. New York: HarperCollins.

Bernhardt, V.L. (1998). *Data Analysis for Comprehensive Schoolwide Improvement*. Larchmont, NY: Eye on Education.

Bernhardt, V.L. and Others. (2000). *The Example School Portfolio, A Companion to the School Portfolio: A Comprehensive Framework for Schoolwide Improvement*. Larchmont, NY: Eye on Education.

Bernhardt, V.L. (1999). *The School Portfolio: A Comprehensive Framework for School Improvement*. (Second Edition) Larchmont, NY: Eye on Education.

Bischoff, Joyce, and Alexander, Ted. (1997). *Data Warehouse: Practical Advice from the Experts*. Upper Saddle River, New Jersey: Prentice Hall.

Brackett, M.H. (1996). *The Data Warehouse Challenge: Taming Data Chaos*. New York: John Wiley & Sons, Inc.

Clark, D.L., Lotto, L.S., and Astuto, T.A. (1984, Summer). Effective schools and school improvement: A comparative analysis of two lines of inquiry. *Educational Administration Quarterly, 20*(3), 41-68.

Deming, W.E. (1993). *Out of Crisis*. Cambridge, MA: Massachusetts Institute of Technology Center for Advanced Engineering Study.

Deming, W.E. (1993). *The New Economics for Industry, Government, Education*. Cambridge, MA: Massachusetts Institute of Technology Center for Advanced Engineering Study.

Drucker, P. (1980). *Managing in Turbulent Times*. New York: Harper and Row.

Education for the Future Webpage. (2000). http://eff.csuchico.edu/

Harrington, J.L. (1998). *Relational Database Design Clearly Explained*. London: Academic Press.

Hernandez, M. (1997). *Database Design for Mere Mortals: A Hands-on Guide to Relational Database Design.* Reading, MA: Addison-Wesley Publishing Co.

Hogan, R. (1990). *A Practical Guide to Database Design.* Englewood Cliffs, NJ: Prentice Hall

Jenkins, L. (1997). *Improving Student Learning: Applying Deming's Quality Principles in Classrooms*. Milwaukee, WI: ASQC Quality Press.

Kimball, Ralph, and Merz, Richard. (2000). *The Data Webhouse Toolkit: Building the Web-enabled Data Warehouse*. New York: Wiley Computer Publishing.

Lezotte, L. (1997). *Learning for All*. Okemos, MI: Effective Schools Products, Ltd.

McGuff, Francis, and Kador, John. (1999). *Developing Analytical Database Applications*. Upper Saddle River, New Jersey: Prentice Hall PTR.

Parsaye, K., and Chignell, M. (1993). *Intelligent Database Tools and Applications*. New York: John Wiley & Sons, Inc.

Parsaye, K., Chignell, M., Khoshafian, S., & Wong, H. (1989). *Intelligent Databases: Object-Oriented, Deductive Hypermedia Technologies*. New York: John Wiley & Sons, Inc.

Petry, F.E. (1996). *Fuzzy Databases: Principles and Applications*. Boston: Kluwer Academic Publishers.

Schmoker, M. (1996). *Results: The Key to Continuous School Improvement*. Alexandria, VA: Association for Supervision and Curriculum Development.

Simon, A.R. (1998). *Data Warehousing for Dummies.* Foster City, CA: IDG Books Worldwide, Inc.

Simon, A.R. (1998). *90 Days to the Data Mart.* New York: John Wiley & Sons, Inc.

Statsoft. (1999). http://www.statsoft.com

Tenopir, C., and Lundeen, G. (1988). *Managing Your Information: How to Design and Create a Textual Database on Your Microcomputer.* New York: Neal-Schuman Publishers.

Teorey, T. (1998). *Database Modeling & Design.* San Francisco: Morgan Kaufmann Publishers, Inc.

The Psychological Corporation. (1955) Test Service Bulletin No. 48.

INDEX